EN CYCLO PEDIA

EVERYTHING YOU NEED TO KNOW ABOUT CYCLING, FROM THE ESSENTIAL TO THE OBSCURE

JOHAN TELL

MITCHELL BEAZLEY

An Hachette UK Company
www.hachette.co.uk

First published in Great Britain in 2018 by Mitchell Beazley,
a division of Octopus Publishing Group Ltd
Carmelite House
50 Victoria Embankment
London EC4Y 0DZ
www.octopusbooks.co.uk
www.octopusbooksusa.com

First published as *En cyklo pedi – allt jag vet om cykling* by
Norstedts, Sweden in 2016
Published in the UK by agreement with Norstedts Agency

Text © Johan Tell 2018
Illustrations © Lukas Möllersten, Lyth & Co

The text on pages 61–68 is based on an extract from *Korsika –
en reseberättelse* (*Corsica – A Travel Story*), published by
Frankofons förlag in 2013

Distributed in the US by
Hachette Book Group
1290 Avenue of the Americas
4th and 5th Floors
New York, NY 10104

Distributed in Canada by
Canadian Manda Group
664 Annette St.
Toronto, Ontario, Canada M6S 2C8

ISBN 978 1 78472 495 5

A CIP catalogue record for this book is available from the
British Library.

Printed and bound in China

10 9 8 7 6 5 4 3 2 1

Commissioning Editor: Joe Cottington
Editorial Assistant: Emily Brickell
Art Director: Juliette Norsworthy
Production Controller: Dasha Miller
Translator: Christian Gullette
Design and Illustration: Lukas Möllersten, Lyth & Co

"THE BICYCLE WILL BE EXTINCT WITHIN THE DECADE"

PJ O'ROURKE, AUTHOR, 1987

FOREWORD

THIS BOOK is my personal and loving tribute to the bicycle and some of the many and varied aspects of cycling. It's built upon my own cycling experiences and on conversations I've had with cyclists around the world.

I've travelled far and wide, despite the fact that "everything" is on the internet now. The net can never replace the experience of seeing a crank punched from metal in an Italian factory, hanging out in a Spanish cycle café, watching tubes being brazed by a British frame builder, or cycling up a French mountain, through New York or across the rocky gravel of a Swedish forest. Nor can I just Google my way to an understanding of the cities that have really chosen to embrace the cyclist, or the feeling in my own garage when I unscrew a bicycle, repair or service it and then manage to screw it back together. Here, I fully agree with the Chinese philosopher Confucius who, in 500BC, said, "I hear and I forget. I see and I remember. I do and I understand."

I've always been someone who cycles, but only when this interest developed into a passion did I become "a cyclist". At the same time, the number of bikes in my garage grew to a number that now causes me to pause when someone asks me how many I have – I always have to count (there are seven, one for each purpose, plus one in reserve and one simply because it's beautiful).

The reason for my greater interest in cycling was four-fold: a new way to get fit that was gentler on my body; an ever-increasing environmental commitment which, among other things, resulted in three books on the subject; a growing aesthetic obsession for a beautiful mechanical machine; and an increasing desire to at least fully comprehend, in our otherwise computerized existence, how something works. This causal four-leaf clover behind my transformation into a cyclist has since grown further. If you're cycling, you'll soon be interested in the surrounding area, and you'll begin thinking about bicycle-friendly road networks and bicycle-friendly, small-scale cafés. The environmental commitment also raises questions about urban planning, who has the right to dominate public space and how best to encourage climate-friendly commuting. The aesthetic appreciation of my bikes is not just about wanting to own beautiful items, but also about identifying what kind of person I am. They symbolize my ideas about democracy, urban planning, child education and a desire for a smaller organic footprint. And the joy of taking apart a bike and putting it back together offers the same feeling of wellbeing as other manual work provides. The homegrown tomato tastes better, the self-knitted sweater is cosier, the garden deck you build yourself provides a greater sense of satisfaction and the bicycle you assemble will soon become so familiar that it feels almost like a new family member.

Having said that, we can't forget that the bike is also a simple and immediate way to create a feeling of wellbeing. Something that Sir Arthur Conan Doyle, the author of, among other things, the Sherlock Holmes books, pointed out a hundred years ago: "When the spirits are low, when the day appears dark, when work becomes monotonous, when hope hardly seems worth having, just mount a bicycle and go out for a spin down the road, without thought on anything but the ride you are taking."

In its simplest form, an interest in cycling can be justified by this basic notion: cycle for a while and it will clear your mind, you'll be happier. You might suggest that cycling should be prescribed by doctors, perhaps, and you'll soon discover that it already is.

Johan Tell

ADVENTURERS on bikes – there have been plenty, in my native Sweden alone. Göran Kropp rode from Sweden to Mount Everest, which he then climbed without support or oxygen. Janne Corax has ridden in hundreds of countries and cycled just over two laps around the world. Renata Chlumska spent 439 days cycling and paddling around the United States.

But maybe it was Englishman Thomas Stevens who started the trend when he began his round-the-world ride from San Francisco on 22 April 1884 on a penny-farthing. His luggage consisted of a belt of money, two shirts, a revolver and a rain cape. Stevens returned to the American West Coast two years later, then wrote a 1,021-page book about his adventure.

ALBERT EINSTEIN in addition to being a scientist, was an extraordinary quotation-machine. His two best-known comments on cycling come, respectively, from a letter he wrote in 1930 to his son and his response when asked about the theory of relativity: "Life is like riding a bicycle. In order to keep your balance, you must keep moving," and "I thought of that while riding my bicycle."

ALFONSINA STRADA was a legendary Italian cyclist – the only woman to complete a stage of the Giro d'Italia. That achievement came in 1924, but it is hard to figure out the story leading up to it in the smoke screen that surrounds her life.

Born in 1891 in a shed outside Modena, her father a day labourer, her mother a wet-nurse, with ten siblings (eight of whom were brothers), Alfonsina learned to ride her father's bike despite villagers cursing her for such sinful behaviour in a girl. She won her first race at the age of 13. The prize was a pig. She broke the world record by cycling 32.58km (20¼ miles) in one hour. She competed in exhibition races all over Europe and even in Russia, where she received a gold medal from Tsar Nicholas II. Her maiden name was Morini, but she married a man who was called Strada, which translates as "road."

She was invited to participate in the Giro d'Italia by the organizer Emilio Colombo, along with the daily newspaper *La Gazzetta dello Sport*. He thought that a female participant would create additional publicity. The male riders, on the other hand, thought it was a gimmick and threatened strikes. Alfonsina was called "The Devil in a Dress" by her male antagonists.

In any case, Alfonsina came to the starting line, slipping through by using the more gender-neutral name of Alfonsin. She left many in her wake, but due to a storm, rain and slippery clay, Alfonsina crashed hard outside Naples and broke her bicycle. In the absence of a support vehicle, it was a long time before a farmer took pity on her and lent her a broom stick with which to mend her handlebars. Though close to her goal, Alfonsina had missed the time limit and was disqualified.

Recently, there has been renewed interest in Alfonsina Strada after the release of an album called *Goodbike*, by the Italian group Têtes de Bois, on which all the songs are about cycling. One of the tracks, *Alfonsina e la Bici* (Alfonsina and the Bike), has a fantastic video featuring the venerable Italian astrophysicist Margherita Hack playing the role of Alfonsina. This isn't as unlikely as it may sound; in addition to her purely scientific publications, Margherita Hack has written books about her life, being among other things, vegetarian, antifascist, a peace activist and opponent of nuclear weapons. One of Hack's last books was her autobiography *La Mia Vita in Bicicletta* (*My Life on a Bike*).

ALLEN KEY is a type of wrench, an indispensable tool for every cyclist. In Italy, the tool is called *chiave a brugola*, in France *clé Allen*, in the Netherlands *inbussleutel*, and in Spain *llave Allen*. Who Allen is or where he comes from, I don't know, but I know that in many countries you can make yourself understood if you make a twisting motion with your hand and say, "Ikea".

ALLEY CAT RACE is an informal bicycle ride held in a city. The first was held in Toronto in 1989 and most participants were cycle messengers. An "alley cat" is a feral city cat.

Usually, the race is held at night and consists of, as in an orientation competition, a number of checkpoints. These checkpoints can sometimes (and this is where they differ from most orienteering competitions) consist of different tasks – physical, mental, alcohol-related – which must be completed before the next stage is begun.

An allcy cat race is quite often, but not always, both informal and in many ways illegal. The first three past the post get the prize, while the final finisher becomes DFL, or Dead Friggin' Last. Legal races occur, but it's a bit like trying to domesticate a feral cat.

ALUMINIUM No one seems to love it. In any case, not as a material for bicycle frames. Exclusive cars may have aluminium bodies, as can aeroplanes and even mobile phones can have a back plate of brushed aluminium. But a bike frame? Nah. However, it was aluminium that ended the reign of steel as the winning material in, for example, the Tour de France. The window of fame for this material was short (it opened in 1995 and closed once more in 1998), but it should have generated some enthusiasts. If so, they're difficult to find.

The first to resist aluminium were the nostalgic steel-lovers who thought that things were better the old way. Then came criticism from those who set their hopes on the eagerly awaited super carbon fibre. It didn't matter to them that the material was lightweight – only one-third of the weight of steel – and rigid. Experimenting with different advanced composites, where aluminium was blended with another metal, such as a ceramic or an organic compound, and imposing names like "metal matrix composite aluminium" didn't even help its case. The material was spurned.

Most cyclists had the unshakable opinion that aluminium frames were big and ugly. And, when they broke, they did so in a strange way – so you couldn't go to the blacksmith and straighten up the frame again as you can with steel. The only time the aluminium frame was... perhaps not "loved," but at least seen as a possible choice, was a few years ago when carbon fibre frames began to come down in price. Then there was the mantra: "Rather a good aluminium frame than a bad carbon fibre one." There were those who thought carbon fibre frames broke in an even stranger way than aluminium ones.

Today, not one of the premium frames is made from aluminium. Just a few years ago, aluminium bikes sold for eye-watering sums. Today, it is almost impossible to find an even remotely expensive one, possibly with the exception of a mountain bike. These days, someone tired of resisting this material can get an aluminium frame from, for example, Dedacciai for a fairly reasonable price. In material and performance, it is the equivalent of the one on which Marco Pantani won the Tour de France in 1998 – the last time a metal frame was included in the prize pool. And if it worked for him, it should be perfectly fine for any happy amateur. It looks good, too.

ASPHALT TATTOO is a permanent reminder of a previous crash on a hard surface. Sometimes, it can look like a ladybird.

ATTITUDE Sometimes I feel everything is about attitude. If society's other road users could change their attitude toward cyclists, everything would be so, so good. But obviously, it's not easy to get everyone else to change their minds.

Let's consider an example of bad attitude. New apartment buildings were put up near me. A sidewalk and a cycle path were created. After a while, the residents complained that cyclists cycled too quickly on the cycle path. So they were complaining about cyclists who cycled legally on a cycle path for cyclists. It's a narrow sidewalk, I realize, but it's not the cyclists' mistake when pedestrians cross their path. Those in charge were not really of the same opinion; they highlighted the cycle path with thick, transverse white markings, so when cycling over them, it feels like crossing a pebble beach. Afterwards you have to feel around your mouth with your tongue to check if any of your fillings are loose. Those who want to ride a bike faster than about 7kph (4½mph) now cycle either on the sidewalk or on the road, where they soon get used to encountering irritated people.

A negative attitude like this arises because pedestrians consider a cycle path to be a kind of extra walkway, and the bureaucrats responsible think the same way. If pedestrians walked out in the road, they wouldn't expect drivers to drive more slowly – and if they did, they wouldn't have any sympathy from others.

Part of the reason for this negative attitude toward cyclists is that it seems to some that cycling is purely a leisure activity. They equate it with a Sunday walk, where the goal isn't important and time insignificant. But those commuting by bicycle aren't just doing it because it's an effective way to beat traffic. In addition to all the health and environmental benefits, the cyclist, like the car driver or those who take public transport, wants to get quickly to work or school, or home to the family. Like those dealing with traffic jams and public transport delays, the cyclist is annoyed when his journey doesn't go as planned, when he can't maintain a steady speed or keep to his planned route. At least as annoying is being told to take it easy and not to cycle as if you're training for an endurance race. Nobody tells a driver to keep to

30 on a 70 road "because you see so much more" and nobody asks a bus commuter to take a later bus because "you'll get there eventually."

I know I'm biased and maybe not seeing things clearly when it comes to traffic cases where cyclists are involved, but it concerns me that, for some reason, cyclists have ended up at the bottom of the list for most town planners. We should have equal priority with other road users, after all.

Those driving a car, as another example, rarely find a bus shelter located in the middle of the road, something that's an everyday occurrence for a cyclist. Motorists rarely find their road dug-up and a sign pointing to a motorway in the wrong direction. Add to that posts and cement bollards, garbage trucks and scooters, construction sites and cement mixers, cars and trucks hogging the road, double baby carriages, skips and trees, dog owners with long leashes and people milling around because they have music in their earphones or are writing a very important text message.

And when I'm forced to slam on the brakes because a food truck with a diesel engine is parked in the middle of the cycle lane, and I make the gesture "But you can't park here" to the driver, and just get back the gesture "Well, where else can I park?", I use the gesture "Try a parking lot – somewhere that doesn't mean parking in playgrounds, dog parks, flower beds or cycle paths," but rarely does anyone understand it.

So, to sum it up, it's not the cyclist's job to solve the problems of other road users by giving up the narrow strip we're assigned for just anything at all, perhaps with the exception of an ambulance or fire engine.

Too many cycle lanes count as a sort of extra space for the needs of drivers, which always come before those of cyclists, because we're at the bottom of the list when it comes to problems with public traffic systems. That's what I mean by attitude. If motorists and pedestrians were exposed to the same things that commuting cyclists experience, those in charge of the public traffic system would immediately be forced to resign.

So what can we do until attitudes change? Why don't others understand that every cyclist often means one less car on the road? That we don't risk killing your child, that we don't use tax-payers' money by taking public transport? (Instead, we cost less tax money because exercise makes us healthy.) Why aren't we celebrated because we don't contribute to global warming? Why don't we get a medal because we make cities quieter? Why are we ridiculed for dressing practically to commute a couple of miles? Why are we chased by police and hated by motorists who look at us like some kind of anti-social miscreants on two wheels?

How do we change the attitude of those who think cyclists only seem to cycle to annoy other road users? I don't know. Sure, there are municipalities working on this. Of course, it makes me happy that a few big cycling projects are underway. I'm a bit of a sucker for a grandiose bike project. Like the beautiful red cycle path snaking through Copenhagen; or the amazing cycle path in Dutch Krommenie, where the coating on the surface is packed with solar cells that power the street lamps and traffic signals and charge electric cars; or the nice bike tunnels in Bath, Antwerp, Rotterdam and San Sebastián. In addition to making it easier for cyclists, these cycling measures say "We like you. We will eventually fix all cycle lanes and crossings, but until then, enjoy these improvements. For this, you are worthy. You are the traffic heroes of everyday life." Then, eventually, maybe the rest of society will also understand that more bicycles and more cyclists are a good thing.

Another measure of bad attitude: in my native Sweden, roughly one in every ten trips is made by bicycle. Of the money invested in traffic, about 0.05 percent goes toward cycling projects, which should be 10 percent. In other words, two hundred times too little.

When did this conflict begin, this battle over the space in our cities and on our roads? Perhaps we can say that it's always existed. Initially, the struggle was between the bicycle and the horse. Cyclists wanted to ride on existing roads and wrote to the responsible authorities asking for more compacted road surfaces. The horseriders wanted a softer surface and regularly got the track loosened by diggers. Then, when horses virtually disappeared from our cities, the struggle between cyclists and motorists began. At that point, roads had long been designed by cyclists. For example, in the United States, the bike organization Good Roads Movement was advocating better roads for their members. Then came the cars. In the United States, newspaper advertisements for revolvers under the heading "The Cyclist's

Friend" appeared, so cyclists could defend themselves against aggressive motorists.

Society would, over time, override and take the driver's side against the cyclist. In most countries, it was mostly about a vision of the future, a future where cars are driven and spacecraft are flown. The bike was thought to belong to the 1930s when hordes of workers cycled to work at the mill. This wasn't the case everywhere though – in some places the opposite was true, most notably in Copenhagen, largely due to the fact that the Danish capital was poor after the war. There, the bike was allowed to remain, where it is still tolerated in traffic, where the government, to this day, supports the bicycle.

A contrasting example is the Essingeleden in Stockholm. A beautiful, arch-shaped highway, held high on pylons, directing traffic around the centre of Stockholm, Essingeleden was opened in 1966. In its conception, the bicycle was almost completely ignored, except for a small half-hearted stretch where a cyclist can barely ride past another cyclist without veering around each other. Cyclists weren't prioritized because there would be no cyclists in the future. That's the way people thought in the 1960s.

The strange thing is that you find the same mentality today. About 15 years ago, the roads in Stockholm were redesigned to include a welcome tram line, yet it would have been quite easy and not too expensive to include a cycle lane. But that isn't what happened. Except for one short stretch which, again, is so narrow that a cyclist can barely encounter a pedestrian without problems. So Stockholm missed a good opportunity to improve cycling infrastructure, yet at the same time it is always saying that it wants to become one of the best bike cities in the world. In Stockholm, eight percent of trips are made by bike; in Copenhagen, the figure is 30 percent.

Therefore, the attitude I'm talking about belongs not just to those who choose to park in the bike lane, but also to those designing traffic infrastructure and roads. The lack of good infrastructure for cyclists is either due to non-existent investment, or simply that it's being built wrong because of ignorance. For example, it can be about cyclist-unfriendly traffic signals: I can cycle along a long road where the driver next to me at each junction has a green light, but I still have to wait and push the button because the signal for cyclists shows red. I can be free-wheeling down a steep hill on a cycle path, only to find that it suddenly crosses a walkway. Or, after cycling over a bridge, I might find that the cycle lane has disappeared altogether, and the signs (I think) are telling me to cycle against the flow of traffic down a one-way street. Car drivers are absolutely unaware of this, and try to intimidate me by honking their horns, flashing their lights and showering me with shouts of, "You don't pay road tax!"

Many of these issues may seem trivial, but that's true about a lot in life. Every time someone parks in a cycle lane and forces us cyclists onto the road, the risk of injury or death increases. The attitude question also impacts when blame is being attributed after an accident has occurred involving a cyclist. The basic reflex is that the cyclist was going too fast, cycled the wrong way, was generally inattentive or not wearing a helmet. All this, despite the fact that statistics clearly show that most bicycle accidents are down to poorly swept, badly maintained or insufficiently salted cycle lanes, or the placing of various hard objects in the bicycle's way.

And when a cyclist dies by falling under a truck, it's not because the cyclist wanted to ride a bicycle alongside trucks, but because there weren't other options. Because the attitude of those responsible was that cyclists should agree to share their space with trucks.

THE BACKSIDE is spared by being lubricated with calendula (marigold) ointment, some say. This "butt-saver" helps prevent chaffing on long rides. A simple calendula salve can be made with beeswax, olive oil and calendula tincture (calendula extracted in a solvent, such as alcohol). Others choose petroleum jelly or chamois cream from Assos or Rapha (chamois is French for the very soft leather used to make bicycle shorts).

Ointments are most needed on long, sweaty rides, or on wet ones, as water increases friction between skin and pants. Some of the tougher cyclists say that ointments are unnecessary, and that the cyclist who has a good saddle and has ridden enough miles on it won't have any problems.

Another type of butt-saver is the small, foldable mudguard called the Ass Saver, which can be inserted under the saddle to stop your trousers getting wet when it's raining.

BACON is cyclist jargon for scabs on your knees, elbows or other protruding parts of your body after a heavy and painful crash.

BALANCE I think of the phenomenon while trying to keep up with a pro coming down a mountain outside Vicenza in Italy. For me, it's fast, but for Angelo Furlan the speed is comfortable. Maybe 50 or 55kph (31 or 34mph). But the wind speed makes it chilly and we've now lost the sun as we're on the north side of the small mountain. So Angelo sits up, lets go of the steering wheel, begins to fumble in his back pocket, gets out his thicker top, puts it on and zips it up. All while we make a long bend at the same speed.

Balance, I'm thinking. It's fascinating that you can cycle as if your bike were steering itself, even if you let go of the handlebars.

As a child, I was always told that the reason a bike could stay upright, even if rolling without a cyclist down a grassy hill, was the gyroscopic effect of the spinning front wheel. More recently I've been told that this is wrong and that a bicycle's balance is due to the "trail". The trail is the distance between the point where an extension of the front fork would meet the ground and the point where the front wheel touches the ground. A significant trail makes the bike want to straighten itself. The longer the trail, the better the balance.

Critics of these theories believe that neither the gyro effect nor the trail play a major role in keeping balance, even when cycling slowly. Today, we talk more about the speed in combination with the cyclist's control as contributing to a bicycle's balance. The importance of that control can be appreciated by anyone who's tried to ride a bike with a manipulated handlebar that turns the wheel in the opposite direction. Then it's almost impossible to keep your balance.

All of these factors probably play a role, with varying importance, depending on the speed. At low speed, the cyclist works a lot with the handlebars to keep balance, but also tilts the upper body, changes the pressure on the pedals, jerks with the hip and knee. Everything to keep the right centre of gravity. The faster the speed, the less these corrections are important, as speed helps keep the balance. And yes, you also get a little help from centrifugal force and the front fork's geometry, the geometry that's best for balance on a touring bike - intended to cycle straight ahead - but worst for an expensive racing bike adapted for a sprinter capable of making abrupt changes and breakthrough attempts. Such a sprinter would be hindered by a bike that wants to continue straight ahead, such a sprinter as Angelo Furlan, shooting down the mountain in front of me while rummaging around in his back pocket for his ear buds.

BALLOON TYRE could have the following definition in any dictionary: "a somewhat imprecise term for all modern low-pressure tyres for pneumatic wheels." One can also add that a balloon tyre is wider than the wheel rim, has a near-circular cross-section, rolls smoothly over uneven ground, but is sluggish. Traditionally, balloon tyres are associated with old military bicycles, which ceased manufacture in the 1980s.

BAMBOO As a material for your bike frame, would it make you nervous? I'd be calm, especially after seeing scaffolding around skyscrapers in Hong Kong made entirely of bamboo. If bamboo can keep workers safe 70 floors above the ground, surely one can trust a bike made of the same material?

A modern bamboo frame is very different to the ones tourists encounter in Vietnam, made of sticks laced together. Today's bamboo is almost as light as a carbon fibre frame, almost as strong and almost as flexible. However, it would also be significantly more expensive. So a person who chooses a bamboo frame probably does it because they are nice or because they have environmental concerns. Bamboo is, of course, a renewable material, which means that when you've worn out your frame, you could say that it's grown a new one, which is the basic criterion for sustainable consumption. But the problem from an environmental point of view is, of course, that the rest of the bike – forks, steering column, seat post, gears, bearings, brakes, pedals, crankshaft, cables – are made from different kinds of metals and plastics. If your only interest is in saving 1kg (2lb 2oz) of plastic, as you probably do when you switch from a carbon fibre to a bamboo frame, it's easier to just stop using plastic bags.

But it's clear, for one who can afford it, that a bamboo frame is a karma healer. The feeling that the frame has grown in a field in Vietnam is probably worth a lot.

But then there are bikes with wooden frames too – even more beautiful and even more expensive.

20

BANDANA was originally a word from the South Indian language Tamil and means "head scarf." This scarf then shrunk and became more like a kind of small hood attached to the neck. It can also be called a "pirate cap" and was made famous in cycling circles by Marco Pantani, also called the Pirate, who wore one over his shaved head (with no helmet).

BAR can, in cycling circles, mean three things:

1. A measuring unit for pressure in bicycle tyres, a source of endless discussion about which one is the only correct one.
2. A synonym for energy-rich, (more or less) useful, individually wrapped, rectangular baked goods kept in a back pocket, which command a kilogram price corresponding to free-range, organic beef fillet.
3. Where one is headed.

BEER is, after 11:00 in the morning, an approved sports drink for those cycling in Belgium.

BEGINNING The beginning took place in 1791 when the French Count Mède de Sivrac invented the bicycle – or, to be more precise, the first two-wheeled vehicle. The bicycle was initially called the *célérifère*, roughly translated as "fast-runner", and consisted of two wooden wheels held together with a wooden section shaped like a horse, a lion, a bird or any other fast-paced animal. The rider straddled his fast-runner and kicked himself forward. Neither of the wheels could move from side to side so the *célérifère* was impossible to steer. The swivel front wheel was introduced in 1817 by Baron Karl von Drais from the Grand Duchy of Baden, who also introduced the shaped wooden beam with a slightly more comfortable saddle.

If this common account is true, every "fast-runner" would have to lift and reposition their bike whenever they encountered an obstacle in order to continue. That sounds a bit unlikely. Which it is. And it's probably not true. Indeed, it has been shown that there was never a two-wheeled *célérifère* at the Palais-Royal in Paris in 1791. Even Count Sivrac may not have existed. The story was the fantasy of the French journalist Louis Baudry de

Saunier who, in 1890, felt that more powerful nationalist articles were needed at a time when the country was still reeling from the humiliating Franco-German war 20 years earlier.

The same can be said of Leonardo da Vinci and his student Gian Giacomo Caprotti; they didn't invent the bicycle either. Their sketches of a bicycle have been proved to be more-recent fakes – something that, however, many Italians have yet to accept.

Baron Karl von Drais's *Laufmaschine*, or "jumping machine", also perhaps has a touch of mythology about it. It's said that von Drais got the idea for his *draisine*, as it was also called, after the terrible famine that hit northern Europe and North America in 1816, caused by climate change after the eruption of the Indonesian volcano Tamboras the year before (1816 was known as "the year without summer"). In addition to the hundreds of thousands of people who starved after the failed harvest, many horses also died. It was these von Drais said he wanted to replace with his jumping machine. Maybe it's true. Or perhaps it was only that von Drais needed a more worthy story because it felt wrong to invent a toy when people were starving. What adds weight to this argument is that the rider became known as a "dandy horse", because most of them were young male socialites who jaunted around in parks without any real goal in sight. It seems his invention was not to save those who suffered from the famine after all.

Interestingly, von Drais' *Laufmaschine* was a rather advanced invention for its time, with its wheels, rear brake and wheel bearings with their brass rings.

BIANCHI'S bicycle factory is one of many units making up the industrial zones that spread out along the Milan-Venice highway. (Well, that's not strictly true: Bianchi is actually located a short way from the *autostrada*, in Treviglio, not very far from Bergamo.)

Claudio Masnata from the Bianchi marketing department meets me by the coffee machine in the entrance hall. A Bianchi coffee machine. "A different Bianchi," says Claudio. "It's one of Italy's most common names, like Rossi."

We go and have lunch at the canteen: pasta with meat sauce, green beans, salad and a piece of taleggio cheese. But no wine.

Claudio was once a professional himself. "I cycled the velodrome, joined the national team for a short while."

"What make of bike did you ride?"

"First a De Rosa, then an SAB, a bike actually made in the tiny little country of San Marino."

"But can the big stars influence which bikes they ride?"

"Well, a Vincenzo Nibali or an Alberto Contador can probably have a say in it. But in general, riders accept the team's decisions."

"How important are the big races – the Tour, the Giro and the Vuelta – for Bianchi?"

"They are very, very important for two reasons. First of all, it is where our products are tested for the first time, hard for three weeks. Secondly, these races offer us our most important media exposure. The Tour de France, for example, is considered the world's third-largest sporting event. But unlike the Olympic Games, the race runs every year. It's broadcast on television in 60 countries."

Claudio pauses to exchange a few words with a couple of passing co-workers. I look out over the Lombardy plain. Nice for relaxed cycling, I think. Nevertheless, there are no cyclists coming from Bergamo a short distance away, where most employees live. You don't do that in Italy. Bikes are ridden on the weekend or possibly after work during the week.

"I had a coach," continues Claudio, "who once said: 'The one who wins a race is the one who makes the fewest mistakes.'"

"Perhaps. But it's a rather sad thought. That the fewest mistakes would triumph over the best training."

"Yes, pretty sad. But it should be the right bike, with the right gears, properly assembled by the mechanic; and the cyclist's diet should be right, the trailer should be located in the right place, and so on. There are many places where mistakes can be made."

We put our food trays on the conveyor belt and head toward the factory. But first we enter a conference room where there is a painting of the old Bianchi factory on Via Nirone (Nirone is the name of one of Bianchi's models) in Milan. It was a huge complex where, in addition to bicycles, cars and motorcycles were also manufactured.

"Bianchi is, today, the oldest European bicycle manufacturer still in operation," said Claudio proudly, then paused thoughtfully for a moment. "But, yes, then came World War II. Production was switched to military equipment, vehicles and bicycles for the army. That's why the factory was bombed hard during the final stages of the war."

The bombs, I think, caused great upheaval; including a curious link between Bianchi's native Italy and my own country – thousands of Italians wound up in Sweden, as the result of an agreement between the countries. Though in truth, it was a deal between industry leaders. In Sweden, the factories were intact and there was a need for labour to meet the growing demand for products, while in Italy, the factories were in ruins and the employees had little to do.

These Italians arrived in their tailored suits, with their handmade Borsalino hats made of finest rabbit hair. They demanded the same salaries that the Swedes received and the same holiday agreements, and they demanded that pasta and canned tomatoes be imported. They also demanded wine for lunch, but that was the limit for the Swedish employers.

One of the Italian families that ended up in Sweden was the Grimaldi family. Born in 1945, Salvatore Grimaldi accompanied his mother to Sweden in the early 1950s to visit her brothers, who had found work at a company called Asea. She loved Sweden so much that she decided to stay, and Salvatore started a grind mill in 1970 at home in his garage in Köping. Three years later, he hired his first employee. By 1982 the first company acquisition was made, followed by many others. Many of the companies he bought were astonishing bicycle factories. Today, they are under the Grimaldi company group, Cycleurope, and include, among others, Crescent, Monark, Gitane, Puch, Peugeot and DBS. Bianchi was bought in 1997.

A remarkable pendulum swing, I think. Italy-Sweden, Sweden-Italy. I now also remember hearing an old radio programme on which Salvatore Grimaldi talked about his life and his rather remarkable career. When it became clear that Swedish Cycleurope had bought one of Italy's most famous brands, it created a national uproar among the Italians. They were upset that, as they thought, everything Italian was now owned by foreigners. But when it became clear that Salvatore Grimaldi was behind the purchase, everyone was calm again. Now it was an Italian who had bought Bianchi, even though he was Swedish. And in Grimaldi's home town of Taranto, far down in the foot of the Italian boot, the newspaper wrote a provincially patriotic

piece about how a proud Tarantonian had bought Bianchi: the same Salvatore Grimaldi who left Taranto as a seven-year-old.

We're now in the factory, which is actually more of a large assembly hall. Here, Bianchi's finest models are screwed together, made from parts manufactured both here and out in the wider world. The simpler models are put together somewhere in Asia and shipped directly to the stores.

"Our best year," says Claudio, "was 1988–89. That year we made four hundred thousand bicycles here and had four hundred employees. Now we have just 80."

In the assembly hall we pass a room for spray painting, in which a lone frame stands in front of an infrared lamp. It doesn't look rational, so I ask what it is. "Ah, that. It is a bike that is going to Gucci."

Now I see that "Bianchi City Gucci" is painted on the frame and it is drying in front of the lamp. If you don't have the brand stamped on the frame, you can get two for the same price. "Most are sold in the United States."

Then we end up in the test lab. In different boxes with Plexiglas windows, bicycle frames are battered by unbearable hammering, bending or twisting robots. "Every fiftieth frame comes in here for testing. It is a quality assurance. Then they are thrown out."

Fabio Ferri sits in the basement and is head of the design department. It's not just about the shape of the bikes, but also their geometry and, nowadays, more about the material they are made from.

"I'm trying to keep up," says Fabio confidently. "Trying to keep track of what is happening in society. What is happening in fashion, what does the latest furniture look like, the cars? A bike is not just sporting gear, it is also an accessory. It has to complement a modern person's perception of himself."

Fabio demonstrates the forthcoming models using a 3D program on his computer and then takes me to a small conference room with a 3D printer. "Everyone thinks it's a coffee machine," says Fabio, opening a small door in the appliance and taking out a blue coffee cup with dishes and spoons made in a single piece. "So I made this for fun. But it's a great machine. Earlier it took weeks for a model builder to produce my prototypes. Now I just press a button and it prints out all the parts of the frame."

The newest thing is a kind of internal system, developed by Fabio Ferri himself, and said to remove 80 percent of road vibration. It's undoubtedly interesting to someone like me whose limbs tend to start to go numb after a while in the saddle. But for now, this venture – called Countervail (CV) or "counterbalance" is being developed for middle-aged athletes. It is supposed to enhance performance.

"When we cannot make the bike easier," Fabio says, "we chose to make the frame less punishing on the muscles. If the muscles can be saved 80 percent of vibration, they have much more power left at the end of a race."

Of course that sounds logical. Fabio produces a small video clip showing two front forks clamped on a vibrating surface. A Plexiglas tube containing a table tennis ball is placed first on the standard carbon fibre fork, and the ball begins to bounce around. Then the tube is put against the new CV fork and the ball is, essentially, still. "Do you see! What a difference. And we have not cheated."

The next person I meet during my visit is Fabio Belotti, creative designer and, therefore, the one who decides how all Bianchi products look. The colours of the bikes, the location of the logos and the club uniforms are Fabio's job, but also the decorative accessories, like wristwatches, jackets and merino wool sweaters in vintage style.

I start by asking about the colour, because even though you can get a Bianchi in several different colours, the brand has its own signature colour. Like a Crescent bicycle should be orange and a Monark blue, a Bianchi should be light green. Though they themselves call it "celest", or sky blue.

"How long has this been the colour?"

"We do not know," says Fabio. "Plus, there are two stories. One is romantic."

"Let's hear the romantic one."

"It is said that when Edoardo Bianchi was commissioned to deliver bicycles to the then Italian royal house, he fell in love with Queen Margherita of Savoy. It's possible he taught her to ride a bike, but we do not know for certain. As a tribute to her sky-blue eyes, he chose to give his bicycles the colour celest."

There is a pizza Margherita too, I think, named after this queen. It's the most boring pizza of all, just tomato, cheese and basil. But I don't mention that. "The second story, the non-romantic one?"

"Well, at one point both the navy and the army had paint that they wanted to get rid of. These discarded paints, the marine blue of the navy and the army grey, were bought by Edoardo Bianchi, mixed together and then used on his bicycles."

Then Fabio shows some sketches of future models. He explains that he works a long way ahead, eighteen months in advance.

"So you work on next year's collection before you know how the collection of the current year was received?"

"Yes, it's difficult. But you see here? No matter what colour the bike is, it always features some detail in celest. It's Bianchi's signature colour. We cannot do without that."

But most of what Fabio thinks up is destined for the bin. "For each model, I may create 20 colour combinations, but only two, three will eventually be produced."

Then he browses through club shirts for an MTB team that Bianchi sponsors. "Whose logo is that?" I wonder and point to something that appears to have been made by an ungifted child with Lego blocks.

"A cement company from here in Bergamo. They are very big."

"New ideas are hard to come by. Difficult for you to put together something nice."

"Yes," Fabio sighs as only Italians can sigh. "It's not easy. Imagine when it was Bianchi linked with Martini. It was beautiful. It was almost impossible to fail. But this? Cement!"

Then it's time for me to go. "Say hi to Stockholm," says Fabio.

BICYCLE KITCHENS exist in many countries, but no two are the same, which is why a precise definition is difficult. One can perhaps say that the idea behind them is a kind of collective ambition to get more people to ride a bicycle.

The person who goes to a bicycle kitchen wants to learn how to repair his or her bike, assemble a bike, or use parts that the kitchen provides. Sometimes it's free, sometimes membership is required, and sometimes you pay for each time you use the facilities. Sometimes the kitchen is supported by an adult education association, sometimes by a city, sometimes by a charity. Sometimes the kitchen receives bicycles from the police's lost property department or from a property company's cellar cleaning. Sometimes the kitchen most resembles a clubhouse for the environmentally conscious middle class, but sometimes it is a vital institution for less-skilled people who need a bike to get to work or school.

A BICYCLE LANE is, as the name indicates, a road for bicycles. In everyday terms, it means a lane running along a street or road separated by a curb, a painted line or a grass strip. This is unlike a cycle path, which is completely independent.

THE BICYCLE PUMP was invented – according to my research – around 1887, at the same time as the air-filled bicycle tyre. What luck! One is quite useless without the other.

Today, there are three main types of valve that the bicycle pump must accommodate: Woods (standard on regular bikes), Presta (found on advanced road bikes) and Schrader (standard on cars and many all-terrain bikes). A good bicycle pump will have three different nozzles to fit the different valve types. An even better one will have a universal nozzle to fit all valves.

For those who want to fix a puncture by the side of the road with as little effort as possible, you can now also buy small gas cylinders containing enough compressed carbon dioxide to fill a bicycle tube. Pumps that you don't have to pump, so to speak.

BICYCLE SHARES New York wakes up. I leave my claustrophobic little room and go out into the July morning. It's already hot. The traffic on 3rd Avenue is dense, heavy and slow. Few bicycles. Here and there a mountain bike, a collapsible Dahon, a racer and a fixed-wheel bike built from an old colourful Peugeot from the 1980s, maybe the occasional cargo bike.

The subway in New York is not to be underestimated in summer time. The sweat beads, the map softens in one's hand, the smell of other people is intrusive. That's why I pick up a bicycle share on 31st Street and shoot down Lexington Avenue. The skyscrapers create shade, the wind cools me. I'm faster than the cars and fresher than the subway riders. That's until I get to the Manhattan Bridge and I'm exposed to the sweltering sun. I leave Chinatown, pedal over the bridge and arrive in Brooklyn as sweaty as a marathon runner. Oh well. I place my shared bike in the little triangular park at Pearl Street and go to my meeting.

Renting a bicycle on holiday is, of course, nothing new. I have done it in Greece and Vietnam, India and Italy. There it was mostly about heading out into the countryside for a while and getting away from oneself, like other tourists. Rarely have I rented city bikes, although I did it in Beijing in 1982 to get around the then almost car-free city and out to the Summer Palace. But the system of bike sharing is something quite new. When I discovered it a few years ago, it quickly became my personal favourite in terms of transport in big cities. As usual with modernity, the phenomenon is older than you might think, and some cities have had bicycle shares for over 20 years. Today, they are in more than seven hundred cities all over the world.

Although the system changes from place to place, there are common factors. Usually you pay a fee and use your credit card as a "guarantee", shedding a few thousand bucks if you wreck the bike. Then you can pick up a bike, head where you're going and drop off the bike in another place. Usually, it's free if you ride for less than 30–45 minutes. The advantages over the older way of renting bicycles by the hour or day are many – in addition to the lower cost. You aren't responsible for the bike when you sit in a café or visit a museum, you don't have to keep track of a return time, and you can borrow a bike 24 hours a day.

I especially appreciated bike shares when I was in London, cycling from Oxford Street to Camden Town (a stuffy underground trip replaced by a pleasant quarter of an hour's cycling), when I explored Andersonville in Chicago, and when I was riding in Copenhagen. The bikes in the Danish capital are equipped with a small electronic device with built-in GPS and map function, so you can – and should – cycle lost, because the bike will help you find your way back.

I leave the Corsican restaurant Le Terroir Corse in Marseille – large ravioli in broth, lettuce salad, stew of wild boar, dessert with chestnuts (the world's best food is made by cooks living abroad and longing for home) – walk fifty metres to a long row of bikes, put in my code, adjust the saddle, and cruise down a steep hill toward my hotel room by the sea a mile away. It feels magical. Partly to roll through a hot French city at night, partly to avoid looking for taxis when buses have stopped, and partly because I have already walked far too much already. It's my last day in Marseille, all my research for a guide book is complete. Tomorrow I travel home but now, thanks to a bicycle share, I enjoy a bike ride along the ocean, warm wind in my hair and the scent of grilled sardines cooked by locals who eat even later than me.

BIKE FIT is a new word for an old science. Users of the term want to make us believe that setting up a bike just recently became a complex matter that needs careful study. Before that, it seems, we were all amateurs, full of doubt, using a tape measure to measure our forearms.

Today, we go to a bicycle shop and spend a couple of hours and a little money to get the bike exactly and scientifically adapted to our own body. And that's okay if you ask me – not least because the stores need all the income they can get in competition with online sales.

But the bike fit that is being studied and sold is actually largely old news. Most advice on how to achieve a perfect and effective seat can already be found in the minutely detailed bicycle bible of 1972, the CONI manual (CONI is the Italian Olympic committee, *Comitato Olimpico Nazionale Italiano*).

To achieve the perfect fit today we use aids like camcorders, pressure-sensitive seat covers, video analysis and motion capture. So a modern bike fit will surely be better than trying to achieve perfection using a 40-year-old printed manual? On Ebay, the CONI manual costs almost as much as a bike fit session – at least that if it has the agreeable cover designed by Italian sports artist Ottorino Mancioli.

BMX derives from "bicycle motocross" and the sport is just that, cycling on a course like one designed for motorbikes.

BMX bikes are short and low, and the saddle is there mostly for aesthetic value as the riders barely sit on them – races are short and heats can last around 30 seconds. BMX has been an Olympic sport since it was introduced in Beijing in 2008.

BMX Freestyle is the stunt-riding side of BMX and includes half a dozen different disciplines, where jumping and performing tricks is more important than racing around a track.

BOB is slang for a female cyclist's boyfriend. The opposite is a Betty.

BOMBING is to cycle, often over a steep precipice, without any regard for one's own safety.

BONE SHAKER is early slang for the first generation of velocipedes. The name refers to the extremely uncomfortable ride caused by the combination of an iron frame and cast-iron wheels.

BROOKS SADDLES are manufactured both as you might expect (in a factory in Birmingham, England) and as you wouldn't expect (in pasture land in northern Europe). In northern Europe, there's a bull in a field. A big bull, heavy in his movements. A little apart from the bull are a few cows and newly born calves – it's May and an apple tree sprinkles its last flowers over this pastoral idyll. This is how a picture of good animal breeding looks. Stone fences, trees that have been shaped by grazing animals, unsprayed fields full of wild flowers, and a bull that is the father of all the calves. What the bull doesn't know is that he will live on long after his death. Or maybe not "live" on, but he will at least be useful, for several decades after his slaughter, and in places far away from this rural idyll.

Let's leave the bull for now and head to London. On Earlham Street, not far from Covent Garden, there have been trendy stores since the 1960s. Now at number 36 we find B1866, and if the name seems cryptic at first, all is revealed when you open the light blue door with the mullioned window panes: it's a shop selling bicycle saddles. On a white-painted brick wall there are about 36 saddles in different colours and with different purposes. That's all. There is also a bicycle and some bags and some retro-inspired clothing available, but the purpose of B1866 – where B stands for Brooks and the numbers for the year when manufacturing began – is to showcase the core products from perhaps the world's most famous saddle manufacturer. Why is that?

I'm on the train to Birmingham hoping to find the answer. From Birmingham New Street train station, I decide to walk along the city's canals, the highways of the early Industrial Revolution. It's fascinating that you can walk on a level below the city itself and stroll for over an hour passing more or less worn brick facades without seeing a single car, just cyclists, and the wish that you had a collapsible canoe about your person.

Steven Green receives visitors in an office that is as thoughtful as the London store is over-designed. A dark oil painting of the founder, a framed photo of a saddle, a clock which is almost right, some pictures in different sizes and different degrees of pallor, which I think show "Employees of the Year", a beige filing cabinet in sheet metal and a carpet that seems to have ignored Allergy UK's advice for the last fifty years. But Steven is nice and immediately opens the door to the factory to show me around. The noise level is high. It hurts; the machines are powered by compressed air and hydraulics. The loud, short, sudden sound of relentless power that cuts, bends or punches holes reminds me of childhood visits to my father's workplace. Like then, I now put my hands in my pockets, afraid of losing any part of me that's sticking out.

Making a saddle is a rather simple procedure: around 20 different pieces are cut from a cow or bull skin, the leather is bleached, moulded in a machine and baked in an oven before having its undercarriage of steel wire and sheet metal stitched into place. And finally, a screw is added, the one that tightens the leather after a bit of use so that the saddle doesn't become banana-shaped.

"But why was it Brooks that survived, because there must have been hundreds of saddle mills in the past," I wonder when we stand next to a man who snaps the copper braces on a Team Pro model.

"I don't know," Steven replies. "Maybe we were just the best." He picked up a B17, just finished, and continued: "This model has been around more than a hundred years, that's a big deal."

Of course. But that's not the complete story. Like most other classic saddle makers, Brooks was once about to be swallowed up by history. The first hundred years went well and the company remained under the same family ownership, but in 1962, Raleigh Bicycle Company bought the saddle maker and operated the company for more than 30 years until even Raleigh had problems and went bankrupt. Then the company passed through the hands of a few more English owners before this revered British gem was sold in 2002 to Italian Selle Royal. It was probably the Italians who saved Brooks from either finally going out of business or seeing their manufacturing moved to a lower-cost site abroad.

Because if the British are good at caring for a well-known brand, Italians are even better at making it profitable. So now Brooks is in Birmingham but, like the Jaguar and Land Rover car brands, which are also manufactured here, the owner is foreign.

We're now coming to the end of the tour and, in the slightly wrong order, have ended up with the incoming raw materials. Here and there, piles of hides, large rolls of chromed steel, copper and titanium wire lie in a corner, with a thick steel sheet in another. There are also lots of drawers containing nuts and screws. It's all that's needed to make a classic saddle.

"Where is the leather from?"

"From many different parts of the world. But everything is vegetable-tanned and dyed. One of the finest leathers actually comes from Sweden. Organic animals that live outside in a cold climate and live a long time, that's when the leather becomes the best and thickest."

"Sweden?" I say a bit surprised when I assumed that the tanning and dyeing of animal skins was something that long ago moved to poor countries. "Do you know where in Sweden?"

"Well, they come from Tärnsjö."

So my next trip will be a shorter one for me, to Tärnsjö, located in the part of Sweden best known for its mosquitoes, and second-best known for making whisky.

"Here are the skins," says Axel Bodén, CEO of Tärnsjö Tanning, and points to some pallets of wet salted leather. "For a bicycle saddle, the skin should preferably come from an old bull. The ancient oxen that were allowed to live a long life because they could at least pull a carriage, hardly exist anymore. In those days you could get skins that were 6mm (¼ inch) thick. Now they are at most 4 or 4.5mm (⅙ inch)."

Then we proceed quickly, while Axel pedagogically informs me about the different methods by which leather is made durable, soft and resistant to moisture.

"The actual tanning," I ask to see that I have really understood correctly, "is only water and dried, powdered tree bark?"

"Yes, we only use plants. In the past, it was oak, spruce or willow. The type of bark also affects the colour. Birch bark makes an almost white leather, while chestnut becomes more and more red. Nowadays we use mimosa the most."

It's the tannins in the bark you need. They are the active ingredients in the tanning process, stopping the leather from decaying. Tannins are also found in red wines. They make a young wine taste stubborn and bitter, but also allow it to be stored for a long time and develop. Some people who think that red wine is good for the health would like to believe that it's down to the tannins, that they're tanned on the inside and thus live longer.

"We stopped using chromium in 1989," continues Axel.

Chromium is a heavy metal which, under certain circumstances, causes an environmental hazard and can increase the risk of allergies and cancers. Most chromium use now takes place in countries with insufficient environmental protections. Now it's on its way from Asia to Africa.

When the tour has finished, I've learned that Tärnsjö supplies its vegetable-tanned leather to companies like H&M, Gants, Haglöfs, Louis Vuitton and Brooks, and it also can be found in children's shoes, car seats, iPad cases and designer furniture.

When I finish in Tärnsjö and start to drive home, that's when I get to see that bull. He who seems to be enjoying life, with no suspicion that he'll live on in the future as 20 exclusive bicycle saddles in another part of the world.

CADENCE is a nice word. A little onomatopoetic. You really hear the rhythm: *ca-dence, ca-dence, ca-dence*. It sounds like what it is: the revolutions of the pedals, *ca-dence*. The pure musicality of the word coincidentally comes from a term borrowed from music. There are several kinds of cadence in music, such as whole, half and false cadence. Common to all of these is that they denote the ending of a phrase, section or whole piece of music. The last damper on the cymbals or the drum. The word "cadence" is also used in equestrian sports and poetry. Anyway. You could also use the word "pace."

Generally, most cyclists have an average cadence of 80–90 revolutions of the pedals per minute, while the professionals may be in the hundreds. All of this is, of course, totally personal. The point of measuring one's cadence is that it can be a good training aid. If you keep your speed the same but shift down a gear, your cadence will lower to maybe 60, and you'll notice that you're increasingly straining the big muscles in your legs as you have to apply more force on each turn if you are doing fewer turns per minute. On the other hand, if you turn up the cadence to around a hundred, it's the heart and lungs that get to work more. Those who choose to ride from time to time at a cadence both below and above the pace that feels most comfortable will eventually become better cyclists. A cadence meter can thus be used in several ways – as a carrot, a stick, or as a means of interval training.

So can music, to return to the word's origin. If you cycle with music in your earphones, you can have track lists with different cadences. To keep a cadence of 90, you'll need a song with 180 beats per minute because you bear down with both the right and the left leg. Three song suggestions: "Objection" by Shakira, "Ring of Fire" by Social Distortion and "Hound Dog" by Elvis Presley. Of course, you can also keep the pace with one leg and choose some less stressful songs at 90 beats per minute.

But how do you know what cadence a song has? Yes, there are – of course – apps for it. For example, Mixmeister and Cadence simply sort your music library for you. You just set the desired cadence and then be on your way enjoying the music the app has found for you. During the course of the ride you can then press plus or minus as the rate changes. If you'd rather sort your library manually, you can use the program www.all8.com. Recently, Spotify launched a collaboration with Nike to automatically tailor the track list you hear during your activities by following your pace.

Of course, you can go old school and find the right songs using a stopwatch and a pen.

CAFÉS catering to cyclists have always existed, but special cycling cafés are a more modern trend.

A couple of steps from Las Ramblas, the tourist-paradise street in Barcelona, lies The Bike Club with its triple business: bicycle shop, workshop and café.

If, not too long ago, I had told my local bicycle dealer that he should expand his business with an espresso machine, learn about air-dried ham and to bake Italian biscotti, he would have looked at me like I was out of my mind. But here we are today.

After looking around, I sit at the bar and order a beer. The bikes for sale are of many different makes. Spanish Orbea, an American Felts model, which looks like an old velodrome bike but now mostly runs like a fixie, Italian Cinelli and the English Brompton. A 20-year-old girl rolls in with her fixed-wheel bike and tells the bartender/salesman/mechanic that her brake lever slips around on the handlebar. He promises to fix it, pours her a beer and heads off to find some shims to solve the problem.

"Nice handlebars," I say.

"You think so? Found them online. Oak. They're dark oak."

Many who have a hobby like to meet other like-minded people. That's why there are so many clubs. When two people meet who enjoy the same beloved hobby, they start writing rules, register membership fees and order clothes with the club's logo. But there are also those who find old-fashioned club activities too demanding and suffocating. They don't feel like going to annual meetings, Wednesday meetings and weekend meet-ups, but still want a sense of community. If you're this type of person and you like bikes, a bicycle café is the solution.

"Did you put the bike together yourself?"

"Well, not really. I ordered the parts and then my boyfriend assembled them."

"There are courses. Don't you have those here?" I ask a new guy behind the beer tap.

"Oh, we did have a bike mechanics course for girls. I've never seen such a collection of muscular girls before."

I let the sexist remark pass, not wanting to destroy the atmosphere in the café by saying something like, "With that attitude, it's no wonder your female football team is falling down the world rankings while your male team is on the way up."

The bike is ready. The woman says goodbye then heads home. Mark, who fixed her bike, turns out to be the owner and tells me about his place.

"We are always here and we have everything. Open at half past nine, close at half past eleven. We repair, sell, rent. Every day we organize a bike ride starting from Plaza España," Mark says, waving his hand a little to indicate where the square is. "Sometimes we have evening tours, too."

"Quite different from the bicycle café I was at in London."

"Which one, Look Mum No Hands?"

"No, Rapha Cycle Club, in Soho."

"Ah, Rapha, no, it's a completely different thing. Rich guys who designed clothes for Team Sky. Expensive."

"Well, it was a strange combo. On the one hand, inviting cyclists to hang their bikes from hooks on the ceiling and watch some racing on television, on the other hand, sales clerks who exuded an attitude of don't-sweat-on-my-merchandise while folding merino wool shirts in small, neat piles."

"Well, I thought so," Mark says in his wrinkled T-shirt with the words "Ride it like you trust it".

"Were you inspired by anywhere in particular when you started The Bike Club?"

My question hangs in the air when Mark's daughter comes in, rolling a fixie with her right hand and holding a small bowl with two goldfish in her left. She places the bowl on the bar, whereupon the other mechanic is immediately there with a Post-it note that reads "Fresh sushi 1€."

"Very funny," says the daughter with a sense of teenage irony, borrowing a lock from her dad and disappearing back into the Barcelona night.

"Not really," says Mark, answering my question, "but I talked a lot with my brother in Australia where cycle cafés are big. What's it like in Stockholm?"

"We have three, as far as I know. Bianchi Café, which was the first, is a trendy place in the middle of the city. Italian slow food, almond biscotti and Sicilian cannoli with sweetened ricotta and pistachios. In the café, the bikes are primarily for decoration and the actual sales and workshop are inside. Everything is refined, tasteful and *molto elegante*. I don't think I could push a bike through the fancy dining room, all sweaty and muddy. Too many suits and dresses to dirty. And just hanging at the bar with a Birra Moretti, that's something I haven't seen many cyclists do."

"A little like Rapha?"

"Yeah, a little. The second, Le Mond, is more of a meeting place for cyclists. Racers and die-hard cyclists. No workshop. No bicycle sales. Devotees. The council has allowed them three car parking spaces for bicycles outside. Rustic. All-you-can-eat-breakfast and the week's soup or vegetarian chilli. Sometimes they have dawn raids at the café. Meet in a suburb at 6:00 in the morning, and depart from there. One stretch is 40kph (25mph), another is slower. You can bring your bike into the café and hang it on the wall and no one turns up their noses at your lycra-clad body as you down a freshly squeezed eco-friendly juice."

"Same atmosphere as this?"

"Yeah, pretty much. The third is a little in between. The Bonne Mécanique is small and intimate, the staff behind the counter hold mechanics courses and warmly advocate the cycling clothes from Café du Cycliste and Après Velo. But..."

This time we are interrupted by two men in black cycle gear, with camel-hump backpacks and cameras mounted on their helmets. They look like the troglodytes in the movie *Delicatessen*, if anyone remembers it. They seem to have cycled through sewers but have probably just gone up and down Tibidabo, the 512m (1,680ft) mountain overlooking Barcelona. The troglodytes say hello, kiss Mark on the cheek and help themselves to a beer from the fridge and some bananas from the bar before settling down on the bench outside the display window.

"Yes," I resume, "many of the cycle cafés I've been to resemble your place, but none more so than Red Lantern in Brooklyn. Same opening hours as you have. No light Italian steel tube furniture, just coarse tabletops straight from the lumberyard, smoothed by years of locals, and semi-precious murals reminiscent of unsightly spray-painted gas tanks on motorcycles. But nice. Locals come in and the guy behind the counter knows your order. Every fifth customer rolls his bike through the highly reluctant door. It seems to need three hands to open it, and everybody seems to think that they'll fix it tomorrow, or whenever. A mechanic who spars with the barista over whether it's to be country music or not on the music system. A lot of fixies, some Italian makes, an obsession for Campagnolo, but also very good American bikes that can carry heavy loads, like Surly and Xtracycle Edgerunner. As a statement against motorization. And every Thursday at 20:30, they have support meetings for those who have crashed or been involved in anything else that needs crisis management."

"Crisis? Sure, that's so New York, huh?"

"I suppose so."

It is getting late. Mark thinks I should come back tomorrow morning to taste Barcelona's best croissants.

"We'll see."

While I'm on the way to my hotel, I'm thinking that there are two problems with cycle cafés having permission to sell alcohol. The first is, of course, that you ride out while not in your right mind, which is stupid. The second is that after a few beers you lose your judgment and buy accessories you had no intention of buying when you stepped in. Like a pea-green suede bicycle seat.

CAMPAGNOLO is almost synonymous with the northern Italian city of Vicenza. Here the company has always been, even though the factory moved from central Corso Padova to modern suburban premises not long ago. Vicenza is in the middle of the Veneto region, with Venice 60km (37 miles) in one direction, Milan 200km (125 miles) in the other and the Alps not far north.

Joshua Riddle points me to the men's toilet in the foyer and says I can change there. In the toilet? Of course, I don't mind, but is this the first time Campagnolo has had a cycling guest?

I am given the bike I am to ride, a handmade Sarto in carbon fibre without any other distinguishing features than Campagnolo's logos. It's equipped with the latest model of the Campagnolo Super Record.

Outside the gates a third cyclist is waiting.

"Angelo Furlan," says Joshua, "You may have heard of him? Former pro."

I nod. Anything else would be cruel.

"Furlan was a sprinter, won two stages in the Vuelta."

"Oh," now I'm really impressed.

Angelo greets me.

"I was a professional until last year. Now I've piled on the pounds," says Angelo, slapping his belly, which doesn't look very big but not exactly a cyclist's stomach either.

Then we come out into Vicenza's industrial areas and the traffic is frenetic and dangerous. Joshua and Angelo don't seem to care. They cycle with space between them, claim their part of the road. No drivers honk.

As we head out of town, the traffic eases. "You have to know where to ride," says Angelo, who did his training rides here for 25 years. "It's a good place. You can ride on the plain if you want, or over the small mountains we are going to today. If you want to climb, we are close to the Alps."

When I'm behind Angelo, I am fascinated by his calves, big as legs of mutton, and it seems to me that those are the muscles that he's using the most. While Joshua is slim, light and riding with a spinning high cadence, Angelo is heavy, has a lower cadence and makes exaggerated movements. He rarely rides smoothly, just stands up and stomps until he shoots away like an accelerating Formula 1 car.

We're on our way to meet this year's participants of The Campagnolo Experience, an event that Joshua started in 2013. The participants first ride in the Granfondo event in Rome, then ride up to Vicenza where the trip ends with a factory visit. Eight days of cycling, a total of 823km (511 miles).

"What do you do now?" I ask Angelo when it's my turn to ride alongside him.

"Ordinary things. Things I never used to do when I toured most of the year. Walking home to my mother's for lunch and eating pasta. Hanging out with my six-year-old daughter. Meeting friends."

After 25km (15 miles) we meet the cyclists who have ridden from Rome. Five enthusiasts from different parts of the world, with two leaders from Thomson Bike Tours, one on a bike and one in a minibus following behind. Joshua, who has met them all before, introduces us. I forget everyone in a millisecond, but meeting Angelo Furlan is a big thing for them. "Are you kidding, two wins in the Vuelta? Cool!"

Angelo tells anecdotes and drops names, describes famous sprints he has participated in and recounts legendary crashes. Especially one with Marco Pantani that everyone else seems to know about already.

"If you look online, you'll see the crash and then, a little bit behind, a guy in blue. That's me."

The group seems to have been doing well. They're happy, happy even though they have spent a whole day cycling through rain and hail. In addition, the group's only woman crashed. She strains over rather uncomfortably to inspect her bandaged leg.

"Leaving prosciutto crudo on the road is a bad way of losing weight," Joshua says, tactlessly.

The girl doesn't understand. She was fishing for sympathy but instead ended up as the punchline of a joke. He meant that her skin looks embarrassingly like dried ham after her contact with the road; she has difficulty seeing any humour in that. She doesn't even laugh when she gets the joke explained to her. She doesn't want to be likened to Parma ham, no matter how world famous it is.

Then we ride back to base over a mountain that I didn't notice on the way out. Extremely beautiful, but tough. I'm falling back in the field. At the top I only have the injured girl behind me. I'm a little ashamed because I didn't let her pass me.

"The Giro sometimes comes up here," says Angelo, "the last climb, then toward the finish in Vicenza. It was always here we finished our training seasons too. Always in these small mountains."

The factory visit begins with Joshua telling the story of when founder Tullio Campagnolo was an amateur cyclist in 20th-century Italy.

"One day during a race in the mountains, Tullio got a puncture in his tyre. It was cold. His fingers were stiff and the wingnut held the wheel tight. He had to hit it with a stone to get the wheel off, which smashed up his fingers until they were bleeding. There must be a simpler way, Tullio thought when he got home, after which he invented the quick release, which is still the standard 80 years later."

And that's how it went. Tullio continued to cycle, won the Tour of Lombardy, the Milan–San Remo race, and then returned to his workshop behind his parents' ironworks to continue with his invention. Joshua shows me an old quick release, decorated with the graceful logo that has recently made a comeback.

"After Tullio invented the quick release, he put in just as much time to make the product beautiful."

Joshua says this as a kind of explanation of why Campagnolo survived while hundreds of other bicycle parts manufacturers were forced to close down. Here, they always combined innovation and quality with an exquisite sense of design. I don't know if this is enough to explain it, but it's true that Campagnolo as a brand has a unique standing in the cycling world – a captivating force that has enticed me to buy bikes with Campagnolo features without actually knowing much about the the brand and, if I can be a little crass for a moment, got the participants of The Campagnolo Experience to empty their wallets just for the opportunity to look more closely at how a chain is made. Campagnolo is a logo cyclists gladly boast about, both on their bikes and on their clothes, and there are those who are so passionate that they have tattooed the company name on their bodies.

"Tullio also invented a bottle opener," says Joshua, who doesn't seem to be able to let up with all the anecdotes. "We still make it. The screws that hold together the opener's parts are the same as those on the Super Record gear."

"I have one of those," interrupts a guy in the group from New York, "but I haven't been able to find the wristwatch."

I don't know what wristwatch he's talking about, but keep in mind that the bottle opener costs several thousand dollars.

We continue around the factory. A large machine eats steel bands from huge rolls and punches them out a dozen different ways. It looks pretty old fashioned. A big contrast to the robot next to it, turning and turning a piece of aluminium, drilling, milling, threading – it explains why there are so few people in the factory. We see a serious man building a disc wheel, a Ghibli. He does one a day, representing that part of the manufacturing that is still pure craft. Ironically, the craft aspect is still found mainly where the most modern material, carbon fibre, is involved. Steel, aluminium and titanium can be machined and joined together by a robot, but carbon fibre is too thin and brittle to suit an automated process. We check out an area that looks practically sterile, where a man picks up a few sheets of carbon fibre from a freezer, irons them with a regular iron and then starts building a carbon-fibre wheel. Then we pass a department with huge water tanks, big like swimming pools, where different metal parts are chromed, galvanized or otherwise treated.

Joshua narrates, explains, and constantly insists that Campagnolo manufactures all the parts, down to the smallest washer, themselves. That everything is manufactured in Europe, albeit a lot now in Romania, but still Europe.

"An important thread running through Campagnolo's history is that we have always been good at developing and working with light metals. NASA came to us before its moon project, and we have recently been able to help medical researchers too. So we usually say that we have not only been to the Champs Élysées, you know the finish of the Tour de France, but also to the moon and inside the human body."

We pass a test unit where a robot is changing gear on a bicycle, first up, then down. That's all it does, every hour of the day, every day of the week. Another machine is battering a front wheel, while a third is pulling on a bicycle chain. Joshua picks up some carbon fibre wheels and explains that they need not become overheated, and actually work well even in rain if they are combined with the right brake pads from Campagnolo. Problems I didn't even know exist because I am not the target audience for these expensive rarities.

We pass small stations where men and women measure with calipers and micrometre screw gauges, look through magnifying glasses and explore with their fingertips. We look into development departments where access is forbidden, where the next generation of gears and brakes are just being hatched.

Now, Joshua is holding a dish with a few small metal cylinders. "These are the new hollow chain pieces. Even there, it was possible to save weight. More than you actually think."

Then we take one last turn past a few larger machines and I realize we won't get to see how the gears are made, which is a pity as they are the company's pride and joy. But it takes too long to assemble all the parts by hand, which is why it is done in Romania.

"The soul," is the last thing Joshua says, perhaps a little bombastic. "A product should be mechanically perfect, have an exquisite design, but it must also be charged with the special Italian Campagnolo soul."

THE CAMPER Hooking up a camper to the rear of my bike isn't really at the top of my wish list. Mainly because of the British film *Sightseers*. There's an enthusiastic cyclist who tours around with his translucent, Plexiglas camper on the back of his bike, rather like a mini caravan. In one of the final scenes, the female protagonist pushes the camper, with the trapped cyclist inside, over a cliff.

Small campers suitable for cycling holidays have cropped up throughout cycling history. From the beginning, these often cigar-like things have often been made from masonite, but there are models in aluminum, various plastics and fiberglass.

The latest versions are large enough for two people and weigh around 40kg (88lb). That's not much for a camper, but compared to a two-person tent, it's a huge increase in weight.

In any case, make sure you don't park near a cliff when there are psychopathic British campers around.

CARBON FIBRE got us cyclists to, if not love, then accept and adopt plastic as a high-quality bike material. It was during the mid-1980s that pure carbon fibre frames seriously broke through – previously, people experimented with the combination of carbon fibre tubes and metal lugs. Manufacturers like Trek and Kestrel were the pioneers, but perhaps also Look, who created a pair of prototype frames for the 1986 Tour de France. American cyclist Greg LeMond succeeded in winning the race on one of those frames. Ironically, on a bicycle with the model name "Bernard Hinault", named for the cyclist who came in second. It was then that carbon fibre had its definitive breakthrough and it would take another eight years before a metal frame won the tour again.

Since Greg LeMond's victory, carbon fibre has not only become cheaper – even within the reach of an amateur wallet – but it has also proved itself for use in more and more bicycle accessories: handlebars, seat posts, rims, brakes, saddles, shoes and more. While other frame materials such as steel, aluminium and titanium seem to be fully developed, carbon fibre is still in a strong developmental phase. We don't

entirely know how useful, rigid, impact resistant and vibration damping this material can be. We also don't know when this product will be eco-friendly and made with raw materials from the forest instead of fossil fuels, but we know it's coming.

The fact that the material is difficult to love is due to some extent on the fact that carbon fibre is just a plastic, it ages in a charmless way, and if it breaks, you can't fix it with the tools found in a reputable garage. In addition, most carbon fibre products are manufactured in anonymous factories in Asia, and not in venerable European workshops where bicycle knowledge has been passed down since the wheel was invented. This somewhat impedes an understanding of carbon fibre, and casts a shadow over its many merits.

I'm not going to offer a scientific explanation here – I'm not capable of understanding it – but in simple terms, carbon fibre is the result of getting carbon atoms to lay parallel in long crystallized wires. The process is old. Edison experimented with carbonizing cotton threads or bamboo fibres to create a good filament for his light bulb 130 years ago. However, it was not until the late 1950s that carbon fibre began to develop into the material we are familiar with today.

The threads produced by the carbon fibre machine are extremely thin, usually between five and ten microns, compared with a human hair, which is about ninety microns. If I understand correctly, it's not very difficult to manufacture simple carbon fibres. What is complicated, which therefore determines the quality of the product, is how the fibre is spun into thicker threads, how they are then woven into sheets, how these sheets are then laid in relation to each other (multiple layers are required) and which binder, usually an epoxy resin, is ultimately used. Epoxy is basically a collective name for a large number of products with huge variations in elasticity, strength and temperature sensitivity. In addition, all epoxy is harmful and environmentally hazardous.

To understand a little more about carbon fibre, I travel to Oxeon, one of the companies behind carbon fibre materials. In the lobby are some surfboards, hockey sticks and golf clubs to show what their carbon fibre material can be used for.

"The latest is Stiga's table tennis bat," said Andreas Martsman after greeting us and leading the way to a conference room.

I'm a little surprised by all the famous brands that their product, TeXtreme, is already used for. Not least because one week ago I had never heard of this company.

"I understand that developing a relationship with a well-known brand makes the rest easier. But where did you start?"

"With F1 cars," replies Andreas.

"But you can't just call Ferrari and say, 'Hello, we have a carbon factory and would like to make your body panels...'"

"Well, that's exactly what we did," Andreas says, pretending it's no big deal.

And while he is looking for an image of an F1 Ferrari, he briefly tells me about Chalmers Innovation business incubator, whose purpose is to assist new technology companies with advice and coaching.

"Do you see?" says Andreas, who now finds the picture and points to the bodywork behind the driver's head. "You see the big-grid pattern. That's our trademark."

"But how many F1 cars use TeXtreme?" I wonder.

Andreas begins reeling-off F1 teams, but then interrupts himself: "Oh, that's probably all of them except for Lotus and Williams. But it's not as strange as it sounds. If an F1 team likes a product on Friday, production may begin on Saturday."

This applies, of course, to tailor-made products that aren't going to be produced en masse.

"We told it like it is. Our product is lighter, by at least 20 percent, sometimes 50, and more durable. TeXtreme can also be much cheaper when it comes to large volumes."

Which is something Ferrari's F1 team doesn't have to worry about, I think.

"More attractive. TeXtreme is also more attractive, and I do not just mean the pattern, but that it is easier to get a beautiful surface finish with our technique. Traditional carbon fibre materials can be a little rough. When BMW chose TeXtreme for their M6 hardtop, that was the reason." Andreas is looking for some bicycle pictures while continuing, "We met Nandan Khokar. He had invented a new way of weaving carbon fibre in broad bands instead of wire thread. Nandan is currently a professor at the local textile college."

The company has found its home in a town with a strong textiles tradition. Initially, they hired space in the basement of a weaving factory and, as weaving in carbon fibre grew while weaving in traditional materials declined, Oxeon expanded by taking over the premises and staff. Now everything is happening in new premises, with venture capital money and great self-confidence behind it.

The first bike built with TeXtreme was a 29-inch mountain bike made by Felt.

"It probably took one, maybe one-and-a-half years before we got a shot at it."

Cycling, explains Andreas, is a good industry to branch into. There, people are really hunting for the things that TeXtreme is good at, like making a product lighter yet more durable.

"A carbon fibre frame consists of between 120 and 150 parts," explains Andreas. "Pieces that fit together like a puzzle into a frame. If the fibres lay in one direction, they are stretch resistant. If they are arranged in another, they are elastic. If they are arranged on a diagonal, they possess a third quality. It is TeXtremes's method of weaving that can create different qualities in the different parts."

In the case of Felt, the Oxeon company's product is already included in most of their major bikes. That's, I think again, fascinating.

But, from a cycling perspective, the biggest success of Oxeon is probably the progress of knighted British cyclist Sir Bradley Wiggins. As he rolled over the finish line as World Champion 2014, he was riding on his Pinarello bike lacquered in the colours of the Union Jack, fitted with Shimano's handmade wheels, which are made from TeXtreme carbon fibre. Campagnolo's Bora Ultra wheels are now also made of a woven material.

CARGO BIKE The cargo bike that stands head and shoulders above all others is called a Bullitt. My neighbour has one. I'm deeply jealous. A Bullitt is like a cross between a racer and a pickup. I see him getting ready to go out, with kids and boating paraphernalia and photo equipment, and think that I'd like to do that too. Although I don't have any photo equipment, boating paraphernalia or children in a size that allows them to be carried in a box on the back of a bike.

I'm travelling to Copenhagen. To me, the Danish capital is the cradle of the cargo bicycle. That is, of course, an inaccurate history and world view because cargo bicycles have been around as long as bikes themselves, and all over the world. In many countries, they are still an important means of transport. I have always associated cargo bicycles primarily with Denmark – not with Vietnam, China or India where they are more common – a fact due solely to Christiania, a self-proclaimed autonomous anarchist area of Copenhagen.

Outside the main train station, I pay for a rental bike and head toward Christiania, pedalling in the opposite direction to all the Copenhagen cyclists who flow through the city in a fierce stream. The tempo is calm. The motor on my electric bike stops helping me at 35kph (22mph). Many of the cyclists around me have electric bikes, nobody is wearing special cycling gear,

far more have very high-heeled shoes as if they are heading off to work as a model and want to arrive in style. A few have cargo bikes, fewer are driving fixies and almost everyone has done something personal with their bike – a bike is rarely just a bike in Copenhagen. No one is cycling at high speed, except the lone bike messengers who zigzag through the traffic, and everyone makes clear signals: stop, left turn, right turn – it looks pretty sweet. This is a considerate cycle country.

Nobody is even wearing a helmet. Which, of course, is not good. But it is beautiful.

Christiania is a sanctuary, a parallel society, formed by a bunch of alternative types in 1971, occupying an area formerly belonging to the Danish Navy. One of the alternative living choices decided by Christiania residents was a car-free society. Since Christiania is fairly large – 84 acres (34 hectares) – and some distance from the centre of the city, 4km (2½ miles) from the main train station, an alternative mode of transport was needed. They chose the bike.

I stop at a Christiania cycle workshop. Outside, a man circles around and around on the gravel and seems to be looking for something, which is probably only in his own mind. A dog walks freely around enjoying himself, and two younger men without teeth have a discussion about a car seat that is facing a bush. It's nice in Christiania, strange houses built and rebuilt for reasons and taste far beyond city architects and architectural review boards, water and greenery everywhere. Exciting craft shops and cool cafés. Nevertheless, I feel – and always have felt – a suspicion that makes it a little uncomfortable. The drug dealer's suspicion: "Are you buying? No? Why are you here then? Are you a police officer? No? Then you *are* going to buy? No? What are you doing here? Bike? Have you come here for a bike?"

Inside the workshop it smells of freshly welded joints and cool steel pipes. It's grim, dark and oily. You almost expect to find some gnomes keeping the forge alight using over-sized bellows. The Christiania bicycle, or Christiania Bike, as it is now called, looks like someone cobbled together a two-wheeled box and welded it onto half a woman's bike. That's probably close to how it was originally designed. In this alternative universe, people transported home-grown vegetables and other goods to town, children to school and kindergarten, tools, construction products, flowers. And they still do, 45 years later. The Christiania Bike is a simple bike built for practical purposes and short journeys in the completely flat landscape of these sprawling marshes. It wasn't on a Christiania Bike that my neighbour came home with half of his cameras or children, because our houses are located on top of a hill.

As I walk around the little workshop, I realize that reality has also reached Christiania. For the bike that once basically had a single, basic model can now be customized with every possible option. A small seat for two little children, seat belts, three gears, five gears, electronic gears, battery lights and a small auxiliary motor mounted on the back. I also realize that the workshop is not about building bikes, just about repairing and modifying. Manufacturing was moved more than 20 years ago to another part of the country. On the one hand, that doesn't feel very alternative, but on the other hand, if you want to spread your alternative lifestyle, as those in Christiania do, you have to expect that others can be just as alternative in a slightly better way.

As I cycle toward the city centre, I pass a shop that sells Nihola, a Danish brand of cargo bike that feels modern and smart, smarter and less hippie-looking than the Christiania Bike, and the same thought returns again. A Nihola 4.0 could be something, I think. It can hold four children under the age of eight, or a load weighing up to 120kg (265lb). Good for riding to the recycling centre, I think.

When the Christiania bicycle was launched, virtually all major bicycle factories had shut down production of cargo bikes. So far, they haven't restarted production, but today there is a fairly wide range of practical bikes being made by small producers. In addition to Christiania's three-wheeled bikes, they also make standard two-wheeled bikes, which are strongly built with sturdy front bumpers or with extended rear bag holders. Their third general style are the bikes known as "Long John" by English-speakers, and *bakfiets* (which means "bicycle") by the Dutch, where the cargo space is located in front of the steering wheel but behind the front wheel, which has moved forward to accommodate it.

In total, there are now more than 100 variations of the cargo bike (according to an excellent compilation by the blogger Cycle Commuter). The current interest in replacing the car with other vehicles for short-haul transport has also made it impossible to find a used cargo bike – I can find only one online at the time of writing.

There is so much to choose from, I think, as I step into a Bullitt cargo bike shop in another part of town. The contrast from Christiania is stark. From forge to showroom, from steel to aluminium, from alternative idea of self-sufficiency to alternative idea of fast-paced city where a bicycle is wiser than a car. And from the thought of a carless society to the idea that car number two is a bicycle.

CHARITY based around cycling is a fairly new phenomenon. Roughly speaking, it can be divided into two categories.

The bike is the new goat. Instead of your charitable donation going to the purchase of an animal, you sponsor a means of transport. Hopefully a poor family who gets a bike can now reach a workplace, a market or a school that was previously too far away. The principle is that the family cycles its way out of poverty.

Alternatively, the bike is a charity magnet. This variant has been around for a long time in countries such as the United States and the United Kingdom, where there is hardly a single cyclist who hasn't cycled, for example, to raise money to find a cure for cancer, diabetes or heart disease. The principle is that you do the cycling and a sponsor pays money to the cause in question and receives exposure on your bike, jersey or along the course.

CHEATING rarely ends in tragedy but, in this case, it did. I'm sitting on the steps of the memorial to the cyclist Tom Simpson. It's a few hundred metres from the top of Mont Ventoux in Provence. I'm on my way down, but I'm not riding any more because the weather is so bad that I'm afraid I'll be blown off the road and down into the valley below. On 13 July 1967, Tom Simpson was heading up the mountain, the thirteenth stage of the Tour de France. But he didn't get any further than here, where he died.

The official cause of death was heart failure due to dehydration and heat stroke, but a strong contributing factor was

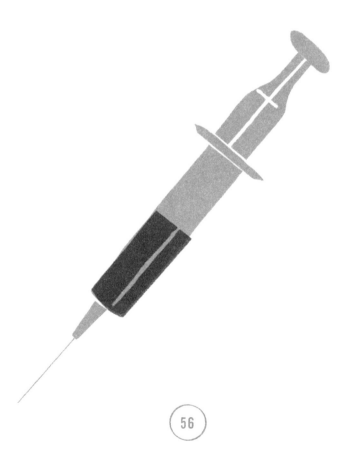

that Simpson had taken the prohibited cocktail of amphetamine and Cognac. Amphetamines began to be used extensively during World War II to inhibit fatigue and hunger in soldiers, so they could march and fight for longer. After the war, ample quantities of amphetamine were still available, and it was sold as an excellent solution for weary shift workers, truck drivers and uninspired students. Amphetamine was also marketed as a dieting agent. I found an old poster online showing a heavy old lady standing in front of a slim mannequin. She's advised to take Tonedron amphetamine preparation three times a day, before breakfast, lunch and dinner.

In the cycling world, amphetamines were permitted until 1965, two years before Simpson's death. The problem for Simpson was that perhaps the greatest benefit of amphetamines is to hide the body's warning signals. In the valley below, the thermometer showed the temperature on this July day to be 45°C (113°F). Simpson had had a stomach upset for three days, and the steep hill he had just climbed was 35km (22 miles) long. In such a situation, using a substance that blocks the body's attempt to say "drink" and "slow down" would of course be fatal.

Simpson had tumbled off his bike five hundred metres earlier but got help from the staff in the team's car. The second time he collapsed was fatal. He died on the spot, only a few hundred metres from the top of the mountain and the downhill that lasted almost to the finish line. In his back pocket he had two empty and one half-empty tube of Tonedron.

The Tour de France started in 1903. The following year, 12 out of the 27 riders completed the race because they cheated – most of them had taken the train.

Among the elite, the motto coined by the father of the modern Olympic Games, Pierre de Coubertin – "The important thing in life is not the triumph but the struggle, the essential thing is not to have conquered but to have fought well" – has never really been respected. Pierre de Coubertin himself won a gold medal at the Olympic Games in Stockholm in 1912. The field was literature.

Those judged as cheats in the past can sometimes lose their guilt when the matter is viewed from a modern perspective. As in the case of Frenchman Eugène Christophe, whose front fork broke as he sped down a steep descent during the 1913 Tour de France, while he was leading the race. In those days, riders were responsible for their own repairs and no one was allowed to help. Christophe had to walk 10km (6 miles), a gruelling two hours with his bicycle over his shoulder, to find a forge where he could fix his bike. It took him three hours to make his own repair, under the instruction of the blacksmith, but still Christophe was penalized because he let a seven-year-old boy pump the forge bellows as he worked.

The most common form of cheating today is medical doping, the history of which can be divided into three phases. The first of these runs up until 1965, when doping was allowed. People had the same attitude toward performance enhancement as we do today toward vitamins. Amphetamine, raisins or a lump of sugar, same, same.

The second phase started in the 1970s with steroid hormones, which mimic natural hormones in the body. The Frenchman Bernard Thévenet later acknowledged that during the 1975 Tour de France – which he won – he had doped with the steroid hormone cortisone, which increases oxygen uptake. At this time cyclists were taking a range of different hormone preparations to improve their performance or to prevent them feeling pain or fatigue. Steroids in cycling were not used, as they are in power sports, to build muscle. The cyclist handled and controlled the doping himself, albeit with the help of team coaches and physicians.

However, during the third phase – which began in 1990 and still continues – doping is done on such a medical level that the cyclist has now surrendered his body to a doping team. The two main methods are blood doping (transfusion) and EPO. Both aim to increase the body's red blood cell count. Because these blood cells carry oxygen from the lungs to the muscles, a higher concentration in the blood can improve an athlete's aerobic capacity and endurance.

In blood doping, some blood is taken from the cyclist, then the red blood cells are removed and stored in the refrigerator. The cyclist's body immediately begins to produce new blood cells. When he has produced a new batch, the original blood cells are returned, thereby increasing the overall number.

EPO (Erythropoietin) is a hormone that simply stimulates the cyclist's bone marrow to produce more red blood cells.

The unpleasant thing about this third phase is that doping has reached a situation similar to that of Frankenstein's monster. The body is handed over for a doctor's experimentation and it can end in a number of different ways.

There is a scene in *Stop at Nothing* - Alex Holme's documentary about Lance Armstrong, the cyclist who was banned for life for doping and lost all his titles hard-won over a 14-year period - which I can't stop thinking about. There are rumours that the doping police are at the entrance, says one of Armstrong's assistants in the film, after which all cyclists are ordered to their hotel rooms. There they immediately destroy their blood samples tainted with EPO and replace them with clean blood. Amphetamine and Cognac seem, by comparison, to be almost honest cheating.

Up on Mont Ventoux, when the wind calms a bit, I wonder if I dare begin my descent down toward Bédoin. Cognac - how can it possibly help you to perform better in a cycle race? If I drink spirits I become relaxed and rather tired.

THE CLASSICS are seven single-day races. A win in one of these makes you immortal. The races are: Milan–San Remo, Tour of Flanders, Gent-Wevelgem, Paris–Roubaix, La Flèche Wallonne, Liège-Bastogne-Liège and the Tour of Lombardy. The latter is the last race of the season, run in the autumn, hence the nickname *la classica delle foglie morte*, "the falling leaf classic."

Some think other races should also be included in this list of classics. That's their opinion.

THE CLAVICLE is often broken in cycle crashes. It breaks if you force the shoulder backward, but can also snap if you try to stop your fall with your hand.

Not having broken your clavicle at least once is considered by many cyclists as a sign of cowardly riding.

THE COMMUTE is a tricky concept. Especially when it comes to commuting on a bicycle. Everyone knows what "commute" means, but nobody can really define it. Least of all, when you want to differentiate commuting from simply riding a bike to work or school. Everyone knows that there's a difference, but what is it? A commute is longer, but how long? Longer than

2km (1¼ miles)? Maybe longer than 5km (3 miles)? A commute definitely takes longer. Is a quarter of an hour long enough, or do you have to ride for half an hour to be a commuter?

Commuters also have a different attitude to their daily cycling than those simply riding to work. They don't commute on an old-fashioned bicycle or a folding bike. They don't commute in the clothes they wear during the day. They know a lot about their bike, know the manufacturer, the number of gears and the width of their tyres. If they are asked, they never answer "it's blue", "I think there's an eagle on the logo", "don't know... it belonged to my grandmother" or "I found it in the trash". In a commuter's brain, there is an ongoing process of self-commuter improvement. Should I switch to narrower tyres, tighter clothes, better lighting, encapsulated switches, or write a blog about rough cycle lanes and deadly drivers?

Actually, you can commute on an ordinary bike, as well as on a racing bike (the riders of which are sometimes called "sports" or "elite" commuters). For beginners, it's best to commute on whatever is available. Often that newly purchased bike can end up on Ebay with the explanation: "Cycled five miles, max, selling due to poor choice."

After commuting for a while, most people end up on a bike somewhere between a racer and an ordinary bike. Some features of each. Thus, relaxed angles, a large number of gears, straight handlebars for a better view of city traffic, with fairly narrow tyres and space for mudguards and knobbly tyres. A good commuter bike should also have a rear rack, or even two, where the cyclist can attach shopping bags on the way home – after all, it would be a bit odd to ride a bike home from work, then go back out in the car to the grocery store.

"CORK?" I think, surprised when I ask the bicycle dealer about what materials his handlebars are made from, and he rattles off all the components. Leather I knew about, silicone and carbon fibre and vinyl, then he continued with some additional synthetic materials. But cork? Oh yes. The dealer brought out some to show me – and it made me happy.

My fascination with cork has more to do with the forests where it is grown. I have walked through Sardinia's cork forests, interviewed a Corsican cork grower who just recently gave up due to a fall in demand, and saw cork mules (not mules made out of cork, but mules that transport cork out of the woods) along the roadside in Andalucía as I cycled past.

So I became the owner of handlebars with cork tape, for the sake of southern European cork forests – and also because they are beautiful handlebars.

CORSICA looks beautiful from above. The helicopter makes a lap around the wind-swept peak of Monte Cintu, snow-covered despite the June warmth, dives into a ravine, follows along its rugged rock walls which, after a short while, become softer and covered with lush greenery, shoots out over the Mediterranean's many shades of blue, swerves back over a bay, hovering above a sailing boat anchored in an idyllic setting. Then the helicopter rises again and veers on.

I'm standing near the harbour in Porto-Vecchio, along with a few thousand others, watching the helicopter's journey across Corsica on a large screen. In two days, the Tour de France cycling competition will start and this is the island's commercial, which will be broadcast all over the world. Like all commercials, it's of course overwhelmingly beautiful and chooses not to tell the whole truth. Nevertheless, I feel that yes, that's what Corsica really looks like, so surprisingly beautiful.

I've been on the island for a month, exploring it by bike and in a car, and found that, apart from some of the suburbs of Bastia and Ajaccio, Corsica is dramatically magnificent wherever you look. But it's actually the number of mountain peaks on Corsica that creates this impression of magnificence. The island is dominated by its mountain range, which runs like a dragon's jagged, ferocious spine right across the island. Wherever you find yourself you can see the mountains, considered by many Corsicans to be the true Corsica, and many of the peaks are snow-covered far into the hot summers.

The large screen continues showing what seems to be every single sight on the island, every bathing spot in every bay, all the ancient houses and every sharp, imposing mountain peak.

The day before, I'd met Marie-Hélène Djivas, who's in charge of Corsica's liaison with the Tour de France. We met on a ferry in the harbour, which seemed to be acting as both a press centre and lodging for the 1,000-plus journalists.

"That was the first problem we had to solve," said Marie-Hélène Djivas. "Corsica is so small. There are fewer than three hundred thousand people living here and in Porto-Vecchio we just don't have the one thousand three hundred extra hotel beds that we required."

It is really small. Corsica's third-largest city has little more than eleven thousand inhabitants, but like everywhere else on the island, the population multiplies by ten in the holiday season, especially during August. Although this year is the one hundredth edition of the Tour de France, it is Corsica's first. The island's only two departments of Pumonte and Cismonte are the last French departments to finally receive the honour to host the race.

"How long have you been applying to host the Tour de France? A hundred years?"

"No," said Marie-Hélène, while she checked one of her two phones that were constantly chiming with notifications. "It was only in 2008 that we applied. It all happened pretty fast after that."

That says a lot about Corsica, that the island is part of France, but still not quite equal to the other regions. They probably haven't applied before because they felt that they weren't welcome. The who-wants-to-go-to-a-ball-at-the-palace-anyway Cinderella syndrome. No one asks about a party that they know they won't be invited to. It's interesting to note that only 10 percent of Corsicans want the island to become independent, yet 50 percent of French mainlanders believe Corsica should be a country in its own right.

When the Tour de France started in 1903, it was set up to promote a sports magazine. Today, just about everything is being promoted by the race, from Russian gas and French lottery tickets to UK TV channels, a Danish bank and the region the cyclists are currently whizzing through.

"So, what is the Tour de France really about? Business, tourism or cycling?"

"All parts are equally important," said Marie-Hélène. "But it is no secret that the competition has an economic aspect. I have seen statistics suggesting that for every cent invested, you get ten, or at least six, back. We think the competition will attract a lot of tourists from Asia and Australia to Corsica."

I nod and think of the couple at my hotel: from Tasmania, sixty plus, flew to Europe, bought a motorcycle and spent three weeks in Corsica, their main reason being the Tour de France passing through.

"With the Tour de France, I think we can improve Corsica's reputation and perhaps attract more investors and extend the tourist season."

I nod again, mainly at the latter. The first time I came to Corsica it was the end of April and the island was strangely empty of tourists. Hotels were closed and restaurants were being renovated, even though the weather was fine and the conditions were perfect for walking and cycling.

Although it's the first time that the Tour de France has visited Corsica, the island is no stranger to bike races. The Tour de Corse started in 1920 and even had professional status between 1971 and 1987, although it is an amateur race again today.

When the Tour de France gets underway, the riders first turn down toward Bonifacio, a route that must have been planned with tourism in mind. Bonifacio is Corsica's picturesque pearl and therefore must appear in the helicopter's footage. Next there's the straight run up to Bastia on the northeast coast. Large parts of this stretch are not so attractive from a tourist's perspective: flat, dry and rather charmless. Although that may seem a little harsh as the beaches are fairly decent and the degree of exploitation in terms of hotels in the area is acceptable, but there aren't any picturesque older buildings here and the mountains are a bit too far away. It would be okay if you didn't know that it was a bit nicer only a few miles away.

The second stage of the Tour de France goes from Bastia to Ajaccio, crossing Corsica's dramatic interior and passing the island's cultural capital, Corte. The winner of this stage came in at an impressive three hours, forty-three minutes and eleven seconds – for me it took two days. For one and a half days I dragged myself up the tough climb. Not super-steep like in the Alps with serpentine roads, but steep enough to force me into the lowest gear. The beauty of the place, however, helped me forgive everything.

It felt like I must have cycled through three climate zones, at least. The first started at the Mediterranean with the maquis: thorny, dense scrub buzzing with insects – an unwelcome

vegetation that no one would voluntarily pass through unless they were on the run from the police. However, the maquis is a blooming spectacle, and also wonderfully fragrant. Napoléon Bonaparte is said to have been able to smell the scent of the maquis on his island of birth when he was imprisoned on Elba about 50km (31 miles) away. It's probably a myth, but doesn't diminish the distinctive and truly unique scent of Corsica. So unique that you can simply cut a large armful of plants in the maquis, distil them and sell the result as *essence du maquis* in the perfume shops.

After the maquis, at a height of about 500m (1,640ft), I realized that I was cycling through woods of tall pines and chestnuts. By 1,100m (3,600ft), these were replaced by beech trees. After that, I endured half a day hanging on the brakes for the longest downhill of my life.

The first time I visit Corte I'm on a bike. In the rain. It's spring and the vegetation comes in 20 shades of green – from bright lime green to lazy olive green. Larks are warbling in the sky, a church bell strikes and proclaims that I have been riding for five hours. It has been a slow ascent up the hill, then quickly down the other side with a happiness that's soon dashed when I realize that I'll have to do this downhill stretch again on the way back up. When the rain stops, my clothes dry quickly in the wind. Generally it's no problem to cycle in the rain, unless you get a combination of rain and windchill. Of course, that's what it's like today.

The day before the start of Corsica's first Tour de France, I manage to get an interview with one of the tour's riders, Fredrik Kessiakoff. The meeting is organized with the help of a tour operator in Porto-Vecchio, Thomas Fourtané.

When Thomas called me, he had managed to get Kessiakoff's mobile number and found out where his team, Astana, was staying.

"See you in twenty minutes."

"Sure," I said, thinking that Thomas had become a more effective journalist than me.

They're so thin, the cyclists, I thought as we wandered around the hotel and looked for Kessiakoff. Not unhealthily thin, just thin like people look in old photos taken in the 1930s. The cyclists' legs were muscular, but not as much as one might think.

The fact that they are thin is not so strange; as Fredrik says when we meet:

"There can be up to a hundred racing days in a year."

A hundred days of competition, where they ride 150-200km (93-124 miles). And just about every other day is a practice day. You'd be skinny, too.

Fredrik was pleasant company and had done well in the Tour the year before, when he distinguished himself as a mountain cyclist and finished second in mountains classification.

"I hope to do as well this year, of course. But there are a lot of factors at play. Partly strong legs, partly luck."

"Luck? Isn't that like when a journalist asked Stenmark if he was unlucky and he replied, 'Isn't it strange, the more I train, the more luck I have?'"

"Yes, of course it is. But it may also depend on what your standing is like. If there is a team in with a chance and I don't pose a threat to the possible victory, I may have the opportunity to break away while the team's assistant rider concentrates on just helping his guy. But we'll see what happens when we get to the first mountain stage, day nine I think it is."

"Day nine?" I wondered a little puzzled. "But before that is the Bastia–Ajaccio stage with the Col de Vizzavona, a pass of 1,163m (3,816ft). Isn't that a mountain?"

My insistence, of course, was due to the fact that I had ridden over that pass – it's the only mountain I've ever managed – and I wanted some praise for it. But Fredrik didn't give up.

"No, that's not a mountain. It's a tough stage, but not a mountain."

Hmmph, I thought, shocked. But later on, when I compare it to the other stages, I can see why Fredrik would think that. It reminded me of the Hugh Grant movie, *The Englishman Who Went Up a Hill But Came Down a Mountain*. Quite the contrary.

Then Fredrik explained that his team wasn't riding to win; their goal was to get their leader in the top ten. A somewhat strange goal, I thought, considering that Astana had just won the Giro d'Italia.

When the second day of the Tour ends in Ajaccio, I'm there waiting. Perhaps my strangest sporting experience ever. For several hours we stand in the crowd under the searing sun watching the race on a huge TV screen, then the cyclists seem to swish past the ends of our noses in two hundred flashes. It's over as fast as a sneeze. Fredrik Kessiakoff has done well, finishing just one second behind the leader.

The riders were preceded by a trail of advertising passing us on the road in front of them. A car with French fries on the roof, followed by one with a tyre on the roof, yet more with cakes, cell phones and ham on the roof. On each roof there was also a cute, frenetic girl. It was all rather embarrassing, like advertising before TV was invented.

When the cyclists ride out of Ajaccio the next day, a stage of just over 145km (90 miles) is awaiting them, including four mountains over 400m (1,300ft) – I know, Fredrik Kessiakoff, you call them hills. This is the most scenic road on the whole of Corsica and familiar to anyone who has come to the island on a motorcycle or as a member of one of the many diverse car clubs that come here. The road meanders and crawls along the rocky cliffs that are as red as the sea below is azure blue. Many cycling tourists also use this road. The bicycle is, for once, the best way of travelling. It's almost impossible to park or even stop if travelling by car here. (But avoid cycling the road the other way, from Calvi to Ajaccio, because it's no fun to meet a truck or German campervan coming the other way when you are on the outside of a bend.) It takes me all day to complete the ride. Up and down mountains. In and out of coves where lone sailing boats sway gently. It's really the most beautiful road I've ever cycled. Everywhere the red rocks have sculptural details. They look like mythical messages left from a distant era. I get a feeling of disappointment when I arrive in Calvi, however lovely the city is. The stage should have ended up in a cave with someone cooking wild boar on a spit over an open fire.

By the time the Tour riders reach Calvi, they have – as I did a few weeks earlier – cycled through large parts of Corsica. And the helicopter which followed the race has sent enticing pictures to all the world's potential Corsican tourists.

CRASHES I particularly remember four of them.

1. I'm a child. It is early summer. June. I'm on my way home from my friend's house. The road is straight. Traffic is sparse. Then I remember nothing until an unknown man rings on our doorbell. My mother opens the door.

"Is this your son?"asks the man holding me in his arms as if I were a bag of potatoes. "He fell off his bike – it's in my car."

At the hospital, the radiologist found that I had a 12cm (5 inch) skull fracture. "We don't use plaster casts on heads," he said, which worried me a little. I was kept in for observation.

The next morning another bed was rolled into my room. In it was my little brother. He had just undergone a planned operation. This coincidence was something we talked about at family reunions for a long time. Imagine, two brothers in the same sick room. A little creepy.

2. I'm a young man, studying. I cycle home at night from another student dormitory to my own. On the handlebars of my green French Motobécane is a plastic bag of LPs (Thelonius Monk, I think) that I had borrowed to record on my tape player. What happens next happens to everyone who cycles with LPs in a bag on the handlebars: one thigh hit the records in the bag, which turned the handlebars by 90 degrees in the wrong direction. A sudden stop.

I fly forward in a wide arc like a character in a cartoon. The bike arcs alongside me because my feet are stuck in the pedal baskets (I was a hipster before hipsters we invented). In a millisecond, everything hurts, but I get back in the saddle again and pedal on. Most importantly, no one saw.

The LPs survived and my ribs eventually healed (if you've listened to any Monk, you'll know I didn't have to laugh very often).

3. I'm an adult. Life is going well. A wife and a summer house. My wife is baking buns while I cycle to fetch the newspaper; that's the arrangement we have. The postbox is 2km (1¼ miles) away.

I pass through a field with five bulls and try to tell myself that it's what people do in the countryside, hang out with bulls. I hop back on my bike and pedal off through the farm. Then I have a gap in my memory. The road sloped down with a small bend, and maybe it was gravelly.

The next thing I remember, I'm in a ditch surrounded by nettles. I get up and cycle off to pick up the paper. On the way back, I stop in the farmyard to say hello to the farmer. He's wondering why my face is so bloody. When I try to explain, I can't get the words out of my mouth. It fascinates me. I see the words inside my head, but my lips are just babbling. Sort of.

Back in the cottage, my wife bandages my wounds, gives me a bun and then goes off to look for my glasses. She finds them in the ditch, which means that I must have been cycling around in a semi-blind state with some sort of concussion.

People in the village still talk about it.

4. I'm middle aged. We're at a fiftieth birthday party. On the way home, we cycle through the woods. It's around midsummer but I've still fitted a new solar-powered light on my wife's bike. She is not a cyclist like me.

The following morning, my brand-new trousers have a 40cm (16 inch) tear in the leg. I myself have a truly enormous bruise in my groin. My wife says I blamed it on a pine branch. The bed is full of pine needles.

CRITERIUM is a kind of bike ride, usually held in a city. It's characterized by a mass start, a short track and high speeds. The Red Hook Criterium has particularly high cult status and uses fixed-wheel bikes without brakes. It takes place in Barcelona, Milan, London and – of course – Brooklyn, where the Red Hook district is located.

CROTCH MEASUREMENT is your inside leg measurement. If you know what it is, it's easier to choose the right size when you buy a new bike, because bikes are sold according to the distance between the centre of the bottom bracket and the top of the seat post. Why it was decided that this measure should be the guide, I don't know, because the seat height is easily adjustable. In my view it would be better to express bike sizes by the length of the top tube as this measure is fixed – the distance you have to reach only changes if you change the stem. But that's the way it is.

The crotch measurement is obtained by standing, in your socks, against a wall and holding a spirit level up between your legs. Fairly firmly, like sitting on a saddle. If you don't have a spirit level, use the spine of a book or a ruler, but these are harder to keep level. Put a mark on the wall. Measure from the floor.

Consider the crotch measurement as a guide only when choosing a bike. You may need a smaller size if you have a short upper body, or a larger size if you have long arms. To make matters even more difficult, different manufacturers use different geometry to make their frames, which is why one brand may suit you better than another. The bike you choose will also be influenced by whether you prefer to sit more upright, or ride further forward, aggressively.

"**CRUISER**" answered the rental guy to my question. "It's a cruiser," he repeated.

"But I reserved a bicycle. A bicycle you can ride on."

"You can ride on a cruiser," said the guy. "They're popular in California. Everybody's got one there."

So I rode away because I had a job to do and didn't want to end up renting a car just because I'd been given a ridiculous bicycle. Really ridiculous. You sit low and lean backward. It had silly, high handlebars and slow-rolling balloon tyres. I cycled along and remembered my childhood Chopper.

British bicycle manufacturer Raleigh launched its Chopper model in 1969. It became an instant success, but only because us kids thought it looked tough – especially kids like me who never got a new bike but inherited older siblings' bikes. A Chopper was considered as much a tough bike as it was a sign of parents who wanted to show that they could afford to buy the newest bike for their children.

For a cyclist, the Chopper was a joke. A small rear wheel and even smaller front wheel, slow cycling, and a tendency to start wobbling at the lowest speed. Uncomfortable, high monkey

bar steering (resembling a hanging monkey, hence the name), a lame saddle to slip off and a gear lever on the frame you could only reach if you let go of the handlebars with one hand. Other manufacturers copied the Chopper and the model is still manufactured today. Other companies, like Schwinn, who made the crazy bike I just hired at the petrol station.

As a phenomenon, these bikes are interesting. It's a fascinating fact that, alongside the mainstream development of the bicycle, where things are always aimed at being better and cheaper, there is a niche where the cycling itself is subordinate to looking cool. So during my 3km (2 mile) ride, I try to tell myself that my awful cycling experience is outweighed by the fact that I look tough. As if I'm cruising along the palm-lined front on Venice Beach in the Pacific Ocean breeze. It's the only way.

CX, cycle cross, has only established itself as a sport in my neck of the woods in recent years. In the rest of Europe, on the other hand, CX has been a fairly big sport for just over a hundred years.

Cycle cross was born in France by road cyclists who wanted to extend the season. It became a way for them to stay in shape from October to February, the period during which road cycling stopped for the winter.

In cycle cross, riders use bicycles similar to regular racers but a bit more robust, with room for larger tyres and the cables on top of the crossbar, instead of below. This is because cyclists often have to carry the bike.

On a Sunday afternoon in November, I'm sitting at a bar in Flemish Oudenaarde, in Belgium. On the screen in the bar, a cycle cross race starts. For an outsider, the sport looks a little strange. The course is short, the terrain is quite level and most of the obstacles are manmade, including some stairs, a bridge, some log paving and something that looks like a long sand jump. The race begins and after just a short time riding, the cyclists jump off their bikes and trek through a stretch of grassland with the bikes on their shoulders. Then they ride a bit further, jump off and run up some stairs. Then they cycle a bit more and come to the sand pit, where some attempt to ride straight through, while others pick their way along the edge. Then they come to some logs, a mound of clay, then back to the flat grassy area where the first lap is complete and a new one begins. The race lasts about an hour.

"What do you think?" Stijn, my tour guide, asked.

At first, I'm tempted to say something about the similarity with Monty Python's *Silly Olympics* sketch, particularly the marathon for incontinents, or the one hundred yards for people with no sense of direction. But I realized I didn't want to be cruel. This is no stranger than a triple-jump or water polo.

"A little strange, that's all," I say carefully.

"Yes, I know," says Stijn. "We laugh at ourselves for this weird sport. Why keep going when it's so muddy – why not just ride a mountain bike?"

A CYCLING SCHOOL BUS is, like a regular school bus, a way to make the children's journey to school car-free and thus safer. A cycling school bus is led by a cycling parent, riding ahead of the neighbourhood's kids and leading them to school.

DATE Twenty-five percent of people in Great Britain responded in a survey that they would rather date a cyclist than any other athlete.

And 27 percent would prefer a cyclist on their pub quiz team than any other type of athlete.

DEATH GRAVEL is grit which has been laid down to give grip in snowy conditions, but remains on roads and cycling paths long after the snow melts. It is one of the biggest causes of cycling accidents.

DESIGNER BICYCLES Here are some models that stand out:

The PARIS GALIBIER was first built by Harry Rensch in the 1940s. The idea behind its unusual frame was to minimize flex, but at the same time increase the elasticity that reduces vibration when riding over a rough surface. The design was recently revived by British bicycle builders at Condor Cycles.

DURSLEY-PEDERSEN. The designer was Danish Mikael Pedersen who moved to Dursley in England, hence the name. The bike is built with a truss construction made from thin tubes, and has a hammock-like saddle. The first version appeared in 1893, was made of wood, weighed 8.6kg (19lb) and set a lot of speed records. Four years later, the wood was replaced with a metal frame. The Christiania manufacturer Jesper Sølling picked up production again in 1978, which is why it's still available today.

The LOTUS TYPE 108 was around in 1987 but was not approved for competitions until 1990. The bike, with its carbon fibre

PARIS GALIBIER

DURSLEY-PEDERSEN

LOTUS TYPE 108

MONOCYCLE

MOULTON TSR 30

monocoque frame and its soft shapes, was a vision of how bicycles could look in the future. During the Barcelona Olympics in 1992, Chris Boardman set the world record on a Lotus Type 108 when he took gold in the 4,000m men's pursuit.

A MONOCYCLE is a bike with only one wheel, which differs from a unicycle in that the cyclist sits inside it. The Brit Ben Wilson wasn't the first to think up the idea. He built his in 2008, but there have been similar patents going as far back as 1860. However, it's undoubtedly great fun.

The MOULTON TSR 30 lies somewhere between fun design and dogmatism, if you can say such a thing about a bicycle. Stylish, expensive, handmade frame in a light construction, folding, drop handlebars, Campagnolo gears, but with 20-inch wheels. For 50 years, this bike has been manufactured on the premise that 20-inch wheels are just as good on the road as larger wheels. No, they aren't! But the manufacturer's tenacity is quite refreshing.

DIRT JUMPING is what it sounds like, jumping over dirt. To start with, mountain bikes or BMX bikes were used to make more or less spectacular jumps over ramps made from soil or gravel, shovelled into a heap.

Today, there are special dirt bikes that resemble BMX bikes with strong front suspension. The sport has gained quite a decent following in recent years because of the spectacular stunts that the dirt riders do, some managing two rotations before coming back down to earth. Nowadays, most competitions use constructed ramps rather than piles of dirt.

DO IT YOURSELF The DIY concept has long been a subject for derision. It describes plucky amateurs, almost always men, trying things they should really hand over to a professional. For a long time, the cycling world was full of do-it-yourselfers. We do-it-yourselfers became rather small-minded when we went into the bicycle shop to buy a spare part or ask for a piece of advice.

But today, the pendulum has, to some extent, swung the other way. The industry wants to include us or, at any rate, make money off us, because each and every bicycle shop now organizes mechanics courses. I went to one of these courses myself. The first night we took the bike apart. The second night we tried to remember where all the parts went (we only just finished before the shop closed for the night).

Being able to tinker with a bike is satisfactory for several reasons. For one thing, a bike is one of the few things in our homes that we can still fully understand and therefore dare to try to repair. And it's an environmentally friendly pastime. You learn to prolong the life of your machine, and you are paying for the knowledge that allows you to do that, rather than paying to consume things.

Those who doubt the merits of a mechanics course by claiming that they can find all they need to know on YouTube undoubtedly have a point. Nevertheless, a video clip, albeit instructive, can't surely be better than an experienced mechanic who knows spokes and bearings, listens to drives and chains, and provides tips such as "to ease the cable in its casing, try widening the opening with an old wheel spoke."

"DRAG, that's what it's all about," says the salesperson, trying to get me to buy a set of aerodynamic handlebars. "At over 30kph (19mph), 60 percent of your power is being used to overcome air resistance."

I don't know whether the salesperson's figures are correct, but the one thing I do know is that if I first look at my bike and then at myself in the mirror, it's pretty clear that the lump behind the handlebars (that's me) is a bigger problem than the design of the handlebars themselves. Nevertheless, I have a bicycle with flattened spokes, internal cabling and a seat post shaped to accommodate the rear wheel. So I can hardly claim to be immune to such talk either.

Like many things related to cycling, it's a question of balance. On the one hand, it's clear that every detail that improves aerodynamics must improve the performance of any cyclist, but on the other hand, these are such small improvements that most cyclists simply won't notice the difference, or feel it's important for them.

I'm reading an advertisement for an expensive new bicycle model. It's said to be 22 watts more efficient than the brand's second-most expensive model. This, says the manufacturer, makes the bike 45 seconds faster on a 40km (25 mile) stretch if you keep up a speed of 40kph (25mph). That's a lot if you're competing in a 30km (19 mile) time trial, but for most of us it's completely irrelevant. Because we don't usually ride that quickly or that far. If you are a time trialler, of course, every watt saved in terms of air resistance is important. Otherwise... not really. It's not even the same for professional team riders, mainly because riding in a pack is so extremely efficient. Just following another cyclist can save you about 25 percent of your energy. If you are the star of a team and get the best position in the pack supported by loyal team members, you can save around 40 percent of your energy ahead of the coming sprint.

I've learned one thing, though. If you have the choice of cycling around a mountain or over the top of it, choose the former, even if the distance is longer. You never get back the energy you put in going uphill when you are riding back down. This is because air resistance increases by the square of the speed. If you double the speed, the air resistance will be four times as high. This means that those of us who ride at a fairly modest pace can get away with chunky handlebars.

ELECTRIC BICYCLE is what it's usually called, but can also be known as an electrically assisted bicycle or an e-bike. It's not to be confused with a moped powered by an electric motor, which you can pedal, but you don't have to, you have to wear a helmet to ride and your vehicle must have insurance. An electric bike, on the other hand, is, as the name suggests, a bicycle where the cyclist gets a little help with the pedal power from an electric motor. While you are pedalling you are charging the battery; if you stop pedalling, what charge you have in the battery will help power the bike. This system is called PAS, which stands for Pedal Assisted System.

There is an ongoing debate as to whether these electric bikes are a good or a bad thing. But it's not a very difficult question to answer. My friend, who has never had a driving licence, rides his electric bike to the golf course. He's more than 90 years old. For him, the electric bike increases his quality of life, and society also benefits as it's probably keeping him healthier – sickness and mobility services being expensive alternatives. But it doesn't just have to be senior citizens who benefit. An electric bike could help a family to take care of all their transport needs – from buying in bulk at the supermarket and taking items to the recycling centre, to transporting a number of toddlers to the nursery – without using a car (*see* cargo bike). Replacing a car with an electric bike is, of course, a big win for the environment.

But if an electric bike replaces a standard bike because the rider is just a little bit lazy, it won't profit the environment or the cyclist's wellbeing. Although the electricity such a bike produces is green energy, that energy has to be saved and batteries still have environmental concerns, both during manufacture and when they are discarded, which is why they should be avoided. But also as important is that it is daily, unassisted pedalling that's so good for us.

ELECTRONIC GEARS are an indulgence I treat myself to when I hire a bike in France. Over two days I'm battling Mont Ventoux, up and down, which, of course, is not the best place to test a gear system because I will probably use just one gear on the ascent and one gear on the descent. But still.

The transmission system works very well. I realize that the precise gear changes also, after a while, give me more confidence to change gear in situations where I would otherwise have hesitated. In particular, under heavy pressure on a steep uphill. Nevertheless, I'm not convinced of the value of electronic gears. I still wrestle with the question: "But why?"

My objections up until now have been that the system is ugly, the idea sounds strange, it is expensive and that batteries always come with an environmental price that should be avoided if possible. In addition, I prefer the idea of mechanical gears because they are something I can fully understand, disassemble, repair and reassemble – which is increasingly rare these days. In fact, I don't really want to be able to connect my bike to a computer to adjust the gears by a few millimetres. However, my feelings against electronic gears are not all that strong and I could easily change my mind if someone gave me a real argument in their favour. If someone could answer my question: "But why?"

When I read other people's arguments in favour of switching to electronic gears, they usually maintain that the power and precision of digital shifting outweighs the mechanical, and that electronic gears are easy to adjust and, once set, you don't have to worry about adjusting them again unless you switch bikes or crash. Also, the performance of an electronic system doesn't worsen over time or in poor conditions, as cables can. So maybe that's a good enough answer. But I can't say that these issues were things I considered a lot and to which I wanted a solution.

Sometimes, when I'm being cynical, I think that the willingness of cyclists to switch to electronic gears is entirely driven by the manufacturers. Mechanical groupsets have – from the manufacturers' point of view – an annoying habit of lasting for decades. That's why they put in so much effort over such a long time to develop this technology – from Suntour's mountain bikes in 1990 to Shimano's launch of its electronic groupset, the Di2, for racing bikes in 2009.

In the world of professional cyclists, new innovations are usually adopted immediately. Partly because they must (it's some of what they are being paid for), and partly to avoid ignoring the new thing then cycling for 30km (19 miles) with a nagging thought that "the others seem to have it easier than me". But there are those who, like me, asked the question: "But why?" Among them is Italian rider Vincenzo Nibali. When he crossed the finish line at the Champs-Élysées in 2014 as winner of the Tour de France, he was riding a bike with a mechanical groupset, Campagnolo's Super Record. He had chosen the old over the new.

Vincenzo Nibali turned his back on decades of development and millions of euros of investment because even Campagnolo's own technicians failed to answer with a good enough reason when he asked, "*Ma perché?*" Nobody wanted to discuss it at Campagnolo's headquarters in Vicenza when I asked the question. The answer I received dodged the issue:

"Manual gears are no better than electronic. Electronic gears are no better than manual. It's a matter of taste."

ENVIRONMENT The environment can be improved by planting a tree. As the tree grows, it absorbs carbon dioxide, the greenhouse gas that contributes to global warming. One usually expects a tree to absorb about 12kg (26lb) of carbon dioxide per year. Different trees, of course, absorb different amounts, depending on the density of the wood.

Those who choose to ride a bike instead of driving a car can help to reduce greenhouse gas emissions too. This is because 1 litre (¼ gallon) of fuel generates about 2kg (4½lb) of carbon dioxide. So those who use a bike to do the 5km (3 mile) round trip to work each day for 24 days can boast the same environmental benefit as a tree offers in a whole year.

But you can, of course, plant a tree as well.

L'EROICA is a non-competitive cycling event that takes place in Tuscany each year, with a vintage theme. Four different routes are offered, varying in length from 38km (24 miles) to 210km (130 miles), the last with a total ascent of 3,700m (12,139ft).

In order to take part, you must fulfil the following criteria:

➤➤ You must ride a bike built before 1987.
➤➤ The bike must have a steel frame (the only aluminium frames allowed are Alan and Vitus, and they must have screwed or glued joints).
➤➤ The gear lever should be on the frame.
➤➤ The pedals should have baskets with straps (clips are not allowed except for Cinelli M71 pedals).
➤➤ The wheels must be low profile and have at least 32 spokes.

There are a few other rules and exceptions, and of course you should wear wool rather than Lycra. At the finish line they serve *ribollita* (a Tuscan vegetable soup), charcuterie, almond cake and – of course – Chianti Classico wine.

The concept is so popular that there are now ten other similar events around the world, including L'Eroica Britannia in England, Cino Heroica in Montana, USA, L'Eroica Japan around Mount Fuji, and Nynäsgirot in Sweden.

EURO VELO is a network of 15 long-distance cycle routes criss-crossing Europe. The plan is that Euro Velo will be complete by 2020, and consist of over 700,000km (435,000 miles) of track.

Already, Euro Velo's map is fascinating to study and will generate wanderlust in those who like to ride far afield. Try route EV1, which passes along the Atlantic coast starting at Nordkap in Norway and ending in Sagres in Portugal; or EV4, which passes through Central Europe, starting in Roscoff in France and ending in Kiev; or EV8, from Cádiz in Spain, along the Mediterranean to Athens. But perhaps the most exciting route, at least for the cyclist with an interest in history, is probably EV13, which follows line of the former iron curtain between what was then East and West Europe. Start in Kirkenäs, Norway, near the Russian border and finish in Rezovo in Bulgaria.

Euro Velo has been set up by the European Cycling Federation.

F

THE FANTOM was a three-wheeled bicycle car. "Was" may not be the right word. It barely existed, except in people's dreams.

The Fantom entered my life in a mail order catalogue from The Hobby Publishing Company, later Hobbex, which showed a drawing of that wonderful machine. It looked like a real car, though smaller, and the catalogue promised that the Fantom was easy to manoeuver, lightweight and fast. Although, of course, it wasn't. Any kid who bought the Fantom (and there were over a hundred thousand of them) was no doubt immediately disappointed. Because it was just a blueprint. And it was a long road between blueprint and finished cycle car, which is why so few were ever seen on our streets.

Today, bicycle cars are usually called "velomobiles". They aren't common. Sometimes, though, I read about an astonishing new world record set by a velomobile with particularly good aerodynamics, for example, a thousand kilometres (621 miles) in 19 hours and 27 minutes. One thing's certain, however. No child today dreams of a bicycle car. Or, at least, not one built from a blueprint sent by a mail order company.

FEMINISM Annie Londonderry cycled out of New York on a fine summer day in 1894. She brought with her a change of clothes and a revolver with a mother-of-pearl grip. Annie called herself an entrepreneur, athlete and globetrotter, and her goal was to cycle around the world.

In Chicago, she exchanged her ungainly woman's bike for a man's sporting bike half its weight. She also swapped her skirt for bloomers – rather like wide, long trousers tied at the ankles. She pedalled away from a husband and three small children, then returned 15 months later and wrote about her escapades in the *New York World* under the signature "The New Woman".

A year later, an older feminist and advocate of the right of women to vote, Susan B Anthony, said the following in a newspaper interview: "Let me tell you what I think of bicycling. I think it has done more to emancipate women than anything else in the world. It gives women a feeling of freedom and self-reliance. I stand and rejoice every time I see a woman ride by on a wheel... the picture of free, untrammeled womanhood."

By this time, women in many parts of the world had started working away from home and some even had factory jobs. The bike, therefore, supported this modern way of living, which helped to make women increasingly equal to men.

I thought about the bike as a feminist instrument when I found myself in Tehran about a hundred years later and talked to a man who ran a hotel on the Iranian island of Qeshm. He thought that more tourists should come to enjoy his island. I replied, as diplomatically as I could, that this could be difficult given the fact that Qeshm has a ban on alcohol, men and women must bathe on separate beaches and women must be fully dressed at all times.

"But women may ride bicycles on Qeshm, yes, on certain bike paths," the man argued, meaning that the island, by Iranian standards, was a shining example of women's liberty.

When Annie Londonderry – who had emigrated from Latvia to Boston and was actually named Kopchovsky – got her alias from her sponsor the Londonderry Lithia Spring Water Company and pedalled on what many contemporary women called her "freedom machine", it was not without protests from conservative parts of society. They thought women should be kept at home under the watchful eyes of men and, furthermore, they considered it medically inadvisable for a woman to ride a bicycle. In the same way that many people in modern-day Saudi Arabia believe that if women drive cars they will damage their wombs and give birth to handicapped children. There were even those in the United States during the 1890s who said women shouldn't ride bicycles because they might become excited by the grinding motion of the saddle. These arguments led to the production of a special "hygienic" saddle, designed to avoid any such excitement.

The last time I saw a bicycle used as a cultural symbol for female liberation was in 2012 when Saudi director Haifaa al-Mansour released her movie *The Green Bicycle*. A nice, simple story about 11-year-old Wadjda's struggle to get a bicycle, despite many objections including medical concerns: "Women who cycle cannot have children." In order to earn money for the longed-for bicycle, Wadjda ironically devotes herself to winning a Koran recitation competition. The film was shot, surprisingly, in Saudi Arabia but was never shown there as the country has no cinemas.

A year after the premiere of *The Green Bicycle*, the powerful Saudi religious police announced that women were allowed to ride bicycles, but only for pleasure, in parks, completely covered up, and in the company of a man.

But the freedom machine rolls on and in Afghanistan, the national women's cycling team are riding hard, despite misogyny, harassment and allegations of corruption.

FILMS in which cycling plays a crucial role in the story:

Il Postino (The Postman) directed by Michael Radford (1994). A bicycling fisherman/postman meets the famous writer Pablo Neruda who is exiled on the small Italian island where the film takes place. A friendship develops. Everyone who has seen the movie wants to ride a bike on the island of Salina, where the movie was filmed, and also perhaps on Capri, where Neruda, in real life, waited for democracy to return to his homeland of Chile. But to be honest, Capri is a rather lousy island for cycling and Salina has only 16.6km (10 miles) of road. But it is certainly beautiful and you can always read poetry there instead.

Jour de Fête (The Big Day) directed by Jacques Tati (1949). This is one of the Frenchman's early masterpieces. A country letter carrier, played by Tati himself, has seen an American newsreel about how the postal service is organized in the United States. Now he wants to do the same in his little French town. Chaos ensues…

My Italian Secret: The Forgotten Heroes directed by Oren Jacoby (2014). This documentary tells the tale of Italian cycling legend Gino Bartali. It was only after Bartali's death that his extraordinary secret was discovered. The fact that he won the Giro d'Italia three times and the Tour de France twice was, of course, no secret. Nor was it a secret that his greatest rival was Fausto Coppi, a fellow countryman but a very different character from him. Coppi was the sophisticated, urban, modern athlete

TATI — JOUR DE FÊTE

while Bartali was deeply religious and felt most at home in the countryside. One of Bartali's nicknames was *Gino il Pio* (Gino the Pious).

Bartali's secret was that, while out on his training rides, he delivered messages for the Italian resistance during World War II. As a national cycling hero, he was allowed to ride a bike and neither Mussolini's fascists nor German Nazis investigated his routes. The truth was that he, among other things, was delivering forged exit visas to Italian Jews so they could escape to safety. We may never know if he really hid the documents in his bicycle handlebars as he does in the film, but by risking his own life, he saved more than eight hundred Jews. The same story is told in Aili and Andres McConnon's book *Road to Valor: A True Story of WWII Italy, the Nazis, and the Cyclist Who Inspired a Nation*.

Breaking Away (1979) is director Peter Yates' contribution to the genre of American films that question small town life. This coming-of-age movie focuses on college cyclists with an obsession for all things Italian.

Ladri di Biciclette (Bicycle Thieves) is Vittorio De Sica's classic 1948 film. It can be summarized as follows: a man, who is completely dependent on his bicycle for work, has his bike stolen. Helped by his son, he searches for it. A classic example of Italian neorealism, the film reminds us of a time when the bicycle was neither a hobby, a workout or a lifestyle accessory. *Bicycle Thieves* often appears on film critics' lists of the world's best movies of all time.

American Flyers was directed by John Badham in 1985, eight years after his success with *Saturday Night Fever*. This film is about two cycling brothers, one of whom is suspected of having a brain aneurism. The film didn't reach the same cult status as *Bicycle Thieves*, even though it starred Kevin Costner in the lead and real professional cyclists from the 7-Eleven team – the team that later competed in the Tour de France, before being renamed Motorola and recruiting cyclists such as Lance Armstrong.

FIXIE is short for "fixed-wheel bike". A fixie is thus a bicycle without a freewheel. If you stop pedalling, the pedals will continue to spin while the bike is moving forward.

The first time I heard of someone who cycled on a fixie, I thought, "Idiot; who came up with something so ridiculous?

Why would you want to reverse progress and cycle without gears and brakes?" You stop a fixie by forcing the pedals to stop spinning, preferably so that the rear wheel skids a bit. Nevertheless, there was something that attracted me to the idea, the reason why it wasn't long before I stood in my garage screwing together what would become my first fixie.

When I think about it, getting a fixie isn't that novel an idea. Lately, the trend in most things seems to be a fascination with vintage versions. As if to say, "things have been going well for far too long. Let's go back to the original!"

Modern-day photographers, tired of 59 sensors and billions of pixels, are now choosing to build their own box cameras and learn to make light-sensitive glass plates. Skiers are digging out generations-old Telemark skis, pulling on climbing gear and forgoing the ski lift. And my friend the Hungarian removed all the features from his motorcycle that he considered unnecessary.

That was many years ago, but there are several similarities between motorcycle and fixie cultures. One summer, the Hungarian and I drove to France on his Moto Guzzi, a real Italian powerhouse. The previous spring, every time we saw each other, he had removed something from his bike. First the indicators disappeared, and then the rearview mirrors. Then the speedometer because, according to the Hungarian, he could tell how fast he was going by checking the tachometer. On the day we departed, he had removed the starter from his bike: "We have to push-start it." Backpacks weren't an option. We lashed a tent to the tank and slept in our leathers.

The same sense of rewinding progress is what makes a fixie so fascinating. If your goal is improvement, there are always new things you can add to your camera or ski equipment, or a new gadget to attach to your motorcycle. If you go in the opposite direction, there's a limit, a minimum, a kind of purity to achieve. When the limit's reached, there's nothing left to simplify. The end goal has been achieved – pure function. That's why I'm unscrewing things I can do without from my bike, or removing them with the grinder, the sparks lighting up the garage.

Nevertheless, the question remains as to who started this fixie trend? I follow the question to New York. I probably could have travelled to Seattle or San Francisco, because trends are rarely created by one person in a single place; there were 22 patents for incandescent bulbs before Edison submitted his own. But in New York, there's a man whose tale is worth telling.

Nelson Vails grew up in Harlem as the youngest of ten children. To contribute to the family's livelihood, young Nelson worked as a bicycle messenger. While travelling to and from clients, Nelson sometimes challenged professional racers training in Central Park. He often won. After one of these tussles, Nelson was talent spotted, recruited by a club and offered a proper velodrome bike. A few years later, he won a silver medal in the 1,000m sprint at the Olympics in Los Angeles. Nelson became the first African American to win an Olympic cycling medal. Sounds like a movie, right? And it became one. The poster from the premiere still hangs in the window of the cultural centre on 116th Street.

When I call Nelson Vails, he's in California but gladly talks about his life. About how he literally cycled out of Harlem and onto every American's television thanks to his Olympic medal.

"I started as a bicycle messenger in the late 1970s. I was an 'OD', an 'original dime', which is someone who started before mobile phones and had to insert a dime in the pay phone to call for instructions for the next assignment."

"Was being a bike messenger helpful to your future career, beyond the obvious benefit of exercising all the time?"

"Absolutely. Riding constantly in New York's fast, tough traffic taught me things that no coach could teach. Now it's easy to laugh at it, but without the bike messenger's daring, there might never have been an Olympic medal."

"Cycling is still a big part of your life?"

"It definitely is. I take part in all kinds of cycling activities and still try to act as a role model for disadvantaged young people. If a poor African American from Harlem can end up on the Olympic medal podium, they can achieve their dreams, too."

"The movie *Cheetah – The Nelson Vails Story* is not the first movie you've been involved in."

"No, the first was *Quicksilver*. Kevin Bacon is still a friend."

From Nelson Vails' childhood home, it's only two blocks to Central Park and some distance from Harlem's poorest areas. Where I stand now, it looks a bit tatty but still okay. However, I think, the neighborhood is still effectively segregated. I see no other white people except those who pass by in double-decker sightseeing buses, filming from the upper deck.

A ramshackle van pulls up in front of the impressive Salvation Army building. On the side of the van there's an advertisement for Miracle Mountain, a Christian resort. A hefty guy gets out and starts talking to a man on the sidewalk whose business it seems is to just stand on the sidewalk talking to people. I'm going to ask if they remember Nelson.

"Oh yeah," says the Miracle man. "I remember him. He won a medal in the Olympic Games. He lived just over there." The man points as if through the block to the next street. "We went to summer camps together. We were the same age."

"Is he still well-known here?"

"Well, I haven't seen him for years."

"What about when his movie came out here?"

"I didn't see it."

"But in the 1980s, wasn't he big?"

"He could really ride a bike," said the Miracle man, avoiding the question.

The man on the sidewalk says nothing, and I'm not sure if he even understood who we were talking about. So I move on.

"Take care," says the Miracle man.

"Have a good one," says the man on the sidewalk.

Not to underestimate Nelson Vails' standing as a role model, but it wasn't his Olympic medal alone that inspired youngsters to ride fixies. Rather, it was the cycle messenger culture that he became part of. Before the profession became hip and was taken over by Europeans looking for seasonal work, bike messengers were largely poor guys from Harlem; they were Latin Americans and African Americans. They wanted bikes that were fast but durable, as well as being cheap. The bikes that met these requirements were often used bicycles, partly because velodrome cycling as a sport was on the downturn, even in the United States. And the velodrome bike is technically a fixie. These bike messengers made a virtue out of necessity. Today, if someone told them to use old gearless and brakeless velodrome bikes, they'd probably laugh.

Then came the movie *Quicksilver*. While Nelson Vails was certainly keen to play himself as the bicycle messenger in the film, it was difficult for an African American to get the lead role in a movie to tell his story back in 1986. Instead, Kevin Bacon plays a young stockbroker who makes a bad investment and ends up losing all the company's money as well as his own. He hits rock bottom but gets a job as a bicycle messenger. There he finds true friendship, love and a rekindled faith in life. Money isn't everything; being able to ride a bike helps.

Many fixies show up in *Quicksilver*, which takes place in San Francisco, but Kevin Bacon didn't learn to ride one, which is why he mostly appears on a Raleigh Competition, a single-speed bike with a freewheel hub and a small brake under the frame.

The other appealing thing about building a fixie is that there aren't any requirements. It doesn't have to be super comfortable, super fast, able to carry a lot of cargo or be a reliable commuter bike. By its very nature it's unnecessary, just for the fun of it, as my saintly mother would say.

So I'm building my fixie myself, with parts I like. The frame is a 30-year-old Crescent that has been standing and rusting in the countryside for the past few decades. The used neon-green front wheel I found on Ebay. The rear wheel is new, bought from my local bicycle dealer, with a sprocket that gives me the 46/17 gear ratio I'm used to. The handlebars I already had laying about in the garage. The handlebar tape – neon-green cork – I bought in Brooklyn, and the saddle in Barcelona.

The rear wheel has a flip-flop hub, by the way. That way, when I eventually realize that riding a fixie is not something for middle-aged guys, I can switch it to the freewheel side and have a small brake mechanism hidden under the frame.

When I finally fit the green, extremely beautiful but somewhat impractical suede saddle I bought in Barcelona, it's deep autumn and rain is hammering on the garage door. It doesn't really matter. I hang my fixie on a hook in the garage and start assembling another dream.

FLAHUTE is French slang for someone, often a Belgian, who enjoys high-speed cycling through heavy rain and thunder over slippery cobblestones while getting splashed in the face by another cyclist's rear wheels. Sort of.

FLÂNEUR CYCLIST is a term used today in the cycling community by those who feel that normal cycling is a little too fast. We don't take the time to idle, saunter or explore our surroundings while out riding.

Most people would associate the word "flâneur" with walking. That hasn't always been the case. Originally, to be a flâneur you didn't have to be on foot as long as you were moving rather slowly and appreciating the things around you. You could therefore walk, ride a bike or even drive a car and still be flâneur. A leisurely idling, without a goal or destination in mind, simply for the pleasure of it. That's why there's a bicycle model, for those who aren't in a hurry, called a Flâneur.

To claim, though, that everyone in the past was a flâneur, meandering along on their bikes, would be untrue. Bear in mind that a penny-farthing could do a terrifying 35kph (22mph).

FOLDING BICYCLE "Take a look at this," my father said sometime in the 1970s. "It's a minibike. It's collapsible." He then took apart the minibike and demonstrated how it could fit into the back of our compact car. Then he screwed it back together again and put it in the garage. There it stayed. I don't remember him ever cycling on it. But it was practical.

Forty years later, I'm the one showing my children a folding bicycle, as they're now called.

"Look, you can fold it up. You can put it in a small bag and hop on the train."

Now mine's in the garage too. This is partly because I work at home and have no job to commute to, and partly because of the strict rules about taking bicycles on the metro. It may also be because folding bicycles are rarely ever practical. Although I've heard endlessly about them from bus commuters with their fancy, folding Bromptons, so I could be wrong. A folding bicycle probably is an excellent invention (*see* Inventions), though neither myself nor my father ever managed to find a use for one.

GEARS James rides in front of me. I'm thinking that he's got better gears than I have. But I'm also thinking how beautiful it is here. Sheep grazing among the cork oak trees, eagles and vultures soaring on high currents and white villages clinging to the mountain sides. Sometimes we pass bulls with long, sharp horns; not surprising as this is *Ferdinand* country. Andalucía, in December.

I'm close to James' rear wheel. Sometimes we're only a few centimetres apart. I'm trying to stay steady to avoid knocking his wheel, when he wobbles. He wobbles a lot. Like me. I'm not staying so close in order to slipstream him; our speed is far too slow up this steep incline. Rather, it's about needing all the motivation I can get to keep pedalling, to keep going. Even to get round just one more bend, especially the tight bends where James always steps it up a bit to get up the incline, which is sometimes 12, 16, 22 percent. It's around these hairpins that James takes off. He just makes up his mind and dashes up the mountain. I see him disappear and at the same time feel myself losing motivation, power and speed. He has better gears, I think, as I try to keep pace.

In sports contexts, we often talk about a winning mindset. About people with a sort of special psyche who always think they can win, no matter how bad the situation is. Often, they manage to do it, too. There are people who give talks about this. Cheerful coaches tell us to "develop a winning mindset at work," trying to tell us that most obstacles are psychological and of our own making. That you can train yourself to develop a winning mindset and avoid restricting, negative thoughts. What these speakers choose not to mention is that those who lose often also have a winning mindset. Of course, there's no psychological difference between the two finalists at Wimbledon, nor between the first

94

and second riders in the Tour de France. Silver medalists have also triumphed over everyone, except the one who took home the gold, but they are rarely described as having a winning mindset.

I myself have a winning mindset, even though I haven't won anything for decades. But I still think about it. When James takes off ahead of me, my reasoning is not that it's because he's 20 years younger than me, an experienced mountain biker and a marathon runner. No, I blame it on the fact that James has different gears on his bike. With the same equipment, I could have challenged him and reached the top of La Paloma first. Rational thinking is not the hallmark of a winning mindset.

When the first bicycles emerged, they didn't have gears. They also lacked pedals and brakes. The rider sat on a shelf-like section between the front and rear wheels, kicked his way forward and had to use his feet like Fred Flintstone to brake and stop.

As the bicycle developed during the second half of the 19th century, pedals were added directly to the front wheel hub. So these bikes still didn't have gears. If you turned the pedals once, the front wheel also rotated a single revolution. The bikes were made with very large wheels, so that you didn't have to pedal like a lunatic.

The modern bike with pedals and chain was invented in 1885 by John Kemp Starley. This had a new feature: the turning of the pedals corresponded to the turning of the rear wheel. The fact that it took about 70 years before it switched from front to rear isn't easy to understand because the phenomenon wasn't new for humanity at all. Anyone who'd ever seen a mill driven by water, wind or a horse knew the principle of shifting rotation up or down to gain higher speed or more power. The Greeks had already understood the principle in the third century BC or thereabouts. Even older is the principle of blocks and chains and pulleys. The origin of these is a little unclear, but we know that about 1,500 years ago, the Mesopotamians were already using such calculations and power transfer to draw water from deep wells. I myself remember being fascinated by my father's demonstration of blocks and pulleys, as well as his words "what you win in power, you sacrifice in terms of control." He'd say that when he let me jack him up to the workshop roof, which made me feel like Superman.

Gears have also existed as a technology longer than people think. At first, people thought that gears were large, clumsy constructions which would be difficult to fit to a bicycle, objections which fail to hold water when you consider the clock, which is a small, light, fine mechanical construction where the force of a spring is converted into precision motion for the hour and minute hands. It's likely, as with all other inventions, that the need for more practical bicycles didn't arise until the late 1800s. It was only then that a middle class emerged and along with it, new ideas about the outdoors and sport. It became fashionable to move, to use one's body to strengthen oneself, but also to explore nature and one's surroundings.

In 1885 when John Kemp Starley presented his "safety bicycle", which looks pretty much like the bicycle we're used to seeing today, he hadn't invented it alone. Rather, it was made from a combination of existing inventions. It was called a "safety bicycle" because you no longer needed to sit 2m (6ft 5in) in the air and steer like you do with a penny-farthing.

It took a few more decades before the bicycle was equipped with more than one gear. The first two-geared model was almost too archaic to be taken seriously. There were two different sprockets, one on each side of the rear hub, one for uphill and one for downhill. In order to change gear, you had to stop, unscrew the rear wheel and turn it over. The gear for cycling uphill didn't have a free wheel. This system is similar to today's flip-flop hubs used by those who want to switch between a fixie and a single-speed bike.

In the 1930s, bicycle gears began to resemble what we're used to today, a mechanism that moves the chain between different sprockets. Remarkably, their development was hampered by the rules of the Tour de France and its organizer, Henri Desgrange. Gears were considered cheating. But in 1937, Desgrange had to give in because cyclists known as *touriste-routiers* – amateur, non-official participants in the race and, therefore, outside the rules of the competition – had acquired bikes with gears and were starting to pass the actual competitors.

The first bikes with gears had only two, but it didn't take long until the number increased to three, four, five. At the beginning, to change gear, the cyclist had to pedal backward while reaching down to adjust a lever on the seat stay, in a similar position to the brake mechanism. It wasn't called the "suicide lever" for nothing. Eventually, the gear lever was moved to a spot above the bottom bracket and then up the down tube, where it remained for

a long time. In 1999, Lance Armstrong chose not to use modern combined braking and gear controls when he rode the Tour de France mountain stage.

When Tullio Campagnolo unveiled his Gran Sport gear system at the Milan bicycle show in 1949, it marked the beginning of the systems we still use today: a cable-operated parallelogram with dual gearshift. The rest is just refinement. Campagnolo hadn't invented this design; he had only made the world's best. Gran Sport was tough and reliable, expensive and, yes, very beautiful.

I'm still behind James, and his gear system is the same overall design as the Gran Sport, just over 60 years later. James has more gears and an electronically controlled switching system, but Tullio Campagnolo, to be honest, was already aware of this technology (and had probably dismissed its battery and electronics as ugly). So, really, it's not James's electronic system I should be muttering about, but his better selection of gear ratios. If you're not used to mountain cycling, this isn't something you often need to consider; you always have more gears than you need and rarely use either the highest or lowest ratio. Looking at older cycling books, they have several pages of tables that show different combinations of chainrings and sprockets and the gear ratios they result in. Today, when most of us have at least 20 gear combinations and change entire cartridges rather than individual sprockets, there aren't many who care about all these calculations. This doesn't mean that you shouldn't think about gears, if only because one day you might be able to pull ahead on a mountain with an average incline of eight percent because you have exactly the right gear ratio.

I try to tell myself that James and I are doing the same work. But the truth is that my lowest gear is way too heavy for my ability. I'm overexerting myself. Of the five cartridges my bicycle dealer could offer me, I went for the middle one where the smallest ring has 12 teeth and the largest 25. The chainrings have 53 and 38 teeth. This means that when I pedalled on my lightest gear (a 39 tooth chainring/25 tooth sprocket combination) I have a 1.56 gear ratio. James has both a smaller, so-called compact chainring and a larger chain sprocket behind, which makes his easiest gear 34/28, a ratio of 1.21. On paper this doesn't sound like much; a few teeth here or there, what difference does it make? However, when I'm behind James, it feels like he spins two easy revolutions while I'm labouring, which allows him to take off, with a difference of about 20 percent between our gear ratios, which is a big difference in this sport of millimeters. We'll overlook the fact that this is all really about James being fitter than I am.

Up on top of La Paloma, James is waiting for me - annoyingly cheerful. He beat me by nine minutes, which - idiotically - spoils my pride in having managed to ride my longest and hardest climb ever, and in a pretty good time too. That's how it is for people with winning mindsets. They'll never be truly satisfied.

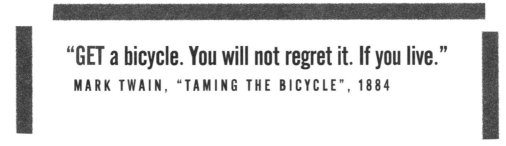

"GET a bicycle. You will not regret it. If you live."
MARK TWAIN, "TAMING THE BICYCLE", 1884

GPS After a long ride, I compare the results on my GPS with that of my teammate who has a device of the same brand. We cycled the route in exactly the same way, except for the inevitable rubber band effect that occasionally occurs.

It turns out that:

➤ He has cycled 1.4km (0.86 miles) less than me
➤ His average speed was 0.7kph (0.43mph) lower than mine
➤ His overall ascent was 652m (2,139ft) higher than mine
➤ His highest peak was 54m (177ft) higher than mine
➤ His deepest valley was 31m (102ft) lower than mine
➤ The ambient temperature for him was slightly higher than for me
➤ He used up 9,171 kilocalories more than me

So these electronic toys, which cost as much as a good used bicycle, didn't provide a single reliable number.

GPS (full name Navstar GPS, the letters meaning Global Positioning System) is a satellite navigation system operated by the US Department of Defense. It was developed in the 1970s but didn't come into operation until 1994.

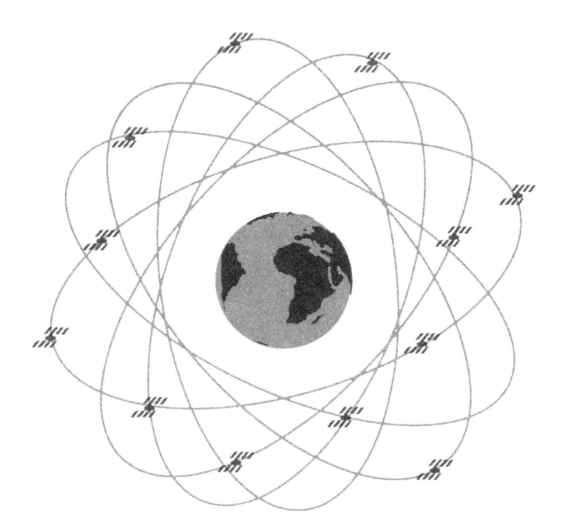

Simply put, a GPS device works by communicating with three satellites at the same time – there are only 27 in all – and the triangulation tells it where it is on the Earth's surface. It can tell me where in the world I am. In order to calculate my altitude, it has to link up with a fourth satellite.

At a bicycle fair, I ask a GPS salesman how it works.

"Yes, there are three satellites which triangulate…"

"Yeah, yeah," I interrupt. "I understand that bit. But how can there be a difference between the readings on two different GPS devices? That's what I don't understand."

"There's a certain margin of error," the salesman says sincerely. "That's why, for example, if you cycled on the surface of the ocean, your GPS might tell you that you were under water, giving you a negative measurement in terms of altitude. And yes, even though I've been standing still all day at this fair, my GPS might show that I have been moving around the neighbourhood."

I understand that there's a certain margin of error. What I don't understand is how, on the other hand, a GPS can be so precise? Every time I stop at a crossroads, whether I'm in Sweden, in Sicily or in Andalucía, I know exactly where I am. Without a doubt. The same way the map service on my computer knows exactly which house I'm in on a street. I'm in number 82, not in 84 or 80. On the other hand, the cycling statistics I compare with my teammate are totally bonkers.

Of course, as an amateur cyclist, it doesn't really matter if the mountain I just cycled up is 207m (679ft) or 150m (492ft) high. I just hope that the GPS on a plane delivers more accurate numbers. But it's exact numbers we GPS nerds are willing to pay a lot of money for. For example, I might want to know whether the incline of a certain hill is more than 16 percent. To the naked eye, it looks somewhere between ten and twenty. But I don't want to pay thousands of dollars for a guess that I could make myself.

Another source of irritation is the map service on my GPS. Yes, it knows exactly where I am, but it's pretty bad at telling me how to get to my desired destination. It's not designed for a cyclist who rarely needs to know how far it is in linear distance, but would like to be able to choose cycle paths, or choose a route without dirt tracks. That's something I can do much more easily using the GPS in my car. The latter feature, according to the salesman, is coming on the next version of my bike GPS.

When riding in a city, the GPS on my bike has an inferior map function compared to my smart phone. The latter uses Google Maps to plot its routes, seems to keep track of most cycle paths, can lead me under, over or around difficult motorway systems, and never tells me how long a stretch is in linear distance. If the battery life of mobile phones improves, as does the system of downloading maps so that you can navigate without being connected to a network (which is currently a pain when you're abroad), the bicycle GPS may find itself obsolete.

Until then, I'll use my bike GPS and kid myself it's giving me accurate data.

GRAND TOURS is the collective name of the three major stage races: the Tour de France, Giro d'Italia and Vuelta a España. All three races follow the same format: three weeks of cycling; seventeen stages; one, maybe two, individual time trials; maybe a team time trial; and two rest days.

All three were founded in the early 1900s. The Tour was first, the Vuelta came last, and in all three cases it was a sports magazine that led the initiative: the French *L'Auto*, Italian *La Gazzetta dello Sport* and Spanish *Informaciones*.

Those who think that sport today is overshadowed by money should remember that ever since the first Tour de France in 1903, the purpose of cycling races has always been a commercial one. Not sport for the sake of sport, but to attract consumers: from the initial goal of selling more newspapers, via the seemingly harmless sponsors like Faema espresso machines, Molteni sausages and Bic ballpoint pens, to today's big businesses such as banks, gaming companies, TV channels, Russian gas companies and investors from Kazakhstan.

Today, Grand Tours are broadcast worldwide, and a good day of the Tour de France can be ranked as one of the most popular sporting events of the year (just below a China–South Korea badminton tournament).

Cycling is no longer just about selling newspapers, and single races can often take place in more than one country. Whereas Grand Tours used to operate solely within one nation's borders, today's races often start in a completely different country. This started with the 1954 Tour de France, which began in Amsterdam.

THE GRANNY GEAR is the easiest gear on a multi-geared bike and, at least partly due to the expression, a gear everyone tries to avoid using, even if they're riding up the north slope of K2.

GRONINGEN is not just the best bicycle city in the Netherlands, it's the best bicycle city in the world. The first cyclist I catch sight of when I exit the train station has a double bass on his back. He whooshes past me as if it were the most natural thing in the world. It's late at night; maybe he's coming home from a gig. I'm looking around for more band members. Perhaps the pianist?

It's a 20-minute walk to my hotel. On the way there, I see more women cycling in fancy clothes than I see cars. Going through Groningen is a bit like being in a movie where the protagonist woke up in another reality. But in this case, it's not inhabited by people from the planet Mars, and it's not somehow always Monday, but rather it's a world without cars. It's the quietest city I've ever visited.

The next day, back at the train station, I'm watching what's going on in the huge underground bicycle parking area. People swish in, park their bikes and sprint to the train. From the train, other commuters arrive, unlock their bikes and pedal away. Two men are going around trying to bring order to the chaos that nevertheless ensues. They stand up the fallen bikes, lift bikes to the upper parking level (there are two levels) to make room on the lower level. Cyclists are going by outside the station on the wide cycle lane, two, three, four, sometimes five cyclists riding abreast. Coming from the station, there are other travellers reassembling their folding bikes as soon as they step outside the entrance. The first thing a visitor to Groningen notices are the bicycles. The cycle lane starts immediately outside the station. The bicycle parking lot is right next to the station, while the taxi stand and the car passenger pick-up and drop-off are both some distance away. There's no doubt: this is a bicycle city with capital B.

Most are everyday bikes – much-used bikes with child seats on the back and sometimes an extra child seat on the frame. Many have panniers or a special storage box on the back, perhaps an old beer crate or, if you're a little more hip, a wooden wine box from a fancy winemaker. A few have sports bikes, and a few have fixies. The bicycle doesn't seem to be a matter of personal taste, just a very good way to get around. Some ride with one hand and hold a phone to their ear with the other. Some seem not to worry too much about steering their bikes if struck by the urge to write a text message that very instant. Yet everything runs smoothly. Everyone uses hand signals. Nobody has a helmet, not even little children. It's clear that in Groningen, the bicycle is not a toy or a piece of sports equipment, but a simple means of transport.

Later, Cor van der Klaauw comes to meet me outside my hotel: sensible bike, luggage rack, dynamo lighting and canvas bags that seem to be a Dutch speciality. He takes off his rain gear, packs it away and suggests a café where we can talk undisturbed.

Cor previously worked as a Cycling Officer, a strange title without much in the way of international equivalent. For a long time, he was partly responsible for the transformation of Groningen into the world's bicycle capital. He throws out some numbers:

"Groningen has about two hundred thousand inhabitants, of which a quarter are students. Nearly 60 percent of all journeys are by bicycle. On average, every resident of Groningen cycles 1.4 times a day. There are three hundred thousand bicycles in the city, far more than the number of residents."

It's truly a world turned upside down. A city where more journeys are taken by bike than by car or bus.

"But how did this happen?" I wonder.

"Mainly for two reasons. The first is that Groningen is a compact city and always has been. Its medieval layout as a small military fortress made the transition to a bicycle city easier. Nearly 80 percent of the population lives within a radius of 3km (2 miles) of the city centre, and 90 percent of workplaces are found in the same area."

"Size plays a roll," I note, thinking about how many cities have this prerequisite. Not many.

"The second reason," continues Cor, "is purely political. In 1972, Groningen was governed by left-wing politicians and they chose to make the city more environmentally friendly. We rode on the waves of the student uprising in Paris and the Club of Rome's ideas about limiting growth. Many may perceive Groningen as car-averse, but that's not true. The idea that permeates everything is that the city should be human-friendly. Accessible to all. On residents' terms. Streets should not be given over to car traffic and car parking. Streets should be as welcoming as people's living rooms. They should be a place to meet, hang out, enjoy yourself. They should be free from fumes and noise. And in this city living room, you should be happy to let your children roam."

Cor shows me some pictures of what this very café looked like in the past, located in an impressive medieval house. The photos show an empty street outside with a bus stop, lined with rows of parked cars. When I look out the window today, I see people strolling, children playing and cyclists. Lots of cyclists.

"How many bicycle parking spaces do you actually have around the station?"

"About ten thousand. All covered. Guarded. They are free. But there are also some indoors where you pay to park your bike. There is also a workshop. The parking areas are open until the last train has arrived, which I think is around two in the morning. Though we now need to extend the parking areas for bikes, probably to double the size. We have an underground bike park in the city centre too, where we can accommodate a couple of thousand bikes."

You can tell that Groningen is a cycling city just by looking at traffic signals. Cyclists may turn right even at red lights, cyclists may cycle the opposite direction to traffic flow on one-way streets, and traffic lights at junctions turn green for all cyclists at the same time, allowing them to turn in any direction without having to worry about cars.

But Cor returns to politics. It's the foundation upon which it is all built. A strong political belief that cycling is the future.

"Needless to say, you need a cycling culture to build upon, but you also need proper investment. For many years now, Groningen has spent four, five million euros a year on cycling infrastructure. It's not enough to have a few cycle lanes here and there to make the bicycle the obvious choice."

"Have you reached that goal?" I wonder.

"Yes. In Groningen it makes sense to travel by bicycle. Psychologically, it feels right, but it is also a real timesaver. In ten minutes you can be in the centre of Groningen. If you take the car, you have to walk to where you've parked it, unlock it, stop at traffic lights on the way and find somewhere to park when you get there. With a bicycle, you just hop on outside your house and pedal away."

H

HAND CYCLES lean against the wall as I step into Vigand Nilsson's premises. One is a racer, while the other is a mountain bike.

"With that I can handle a 20 percent slope," says Vigand, pointing to the mountain bike. "It's the one I use most. There are fewer conflicts when I cycle in the forest."

Two wheels or three wheels, leg cycle or hand cycle, cyclists' experiences in traffic always seem to be the same.

"The cycle paths are built for a maximum speed of 15kph (9mph)," continues Vigand. "Way too slow for me. But when I choose to ride on the road instead, car drivers get annoyed."

Vigand continues to talk about watts (the energy you put into turning the pedals), about weight, about his new crankset, which flexes very little, and about aerodynamics.

"I have a cycling route. About 4km (2½ miles). I cycle round it at the same wattage, usually 170, change some detail on the bike, then cycle the route again to see if there's any time gain."

The company is called TiArrow; "Ti" stands for titanium, a material Vigand has worked with for more than 20 years. He not only builds hand bicycles but also wheelchairs and regular bicycles, which he calls "leg cycles." He has just put two beautiful titanium frames for sale online – that's how I found him.

"I thought they would be sold immediately. But no one has enquired. No one!"

"It's all about the brand. Yours is small and fairly unknown."

"Yeah, I should spend a couple of years trying to build the brand. But I don't have time for that."

Vigand tells me about the fantastic properties of titanium. About how, properly used and in combination with carbon fibre, it produces a product with outstanding performance.

"But look," I say, "your road bike is extremely low. You have to ride it almost lying flat. Can you see anything at all?"

"Actually, it's true. The problem is that the bottom bracket obscures your vision."

The bicycles are designed here, welded in China and then returned to be assembled and delivered. Vigand shows me one of his bikes - 7.5kg (16½lb) when it's race ready - which has been ordered by a former US Paralympic, a guy Vigand himself competed against in the World Cup a few years ago.

"The Chinese are very good at welding bicycles. Strangely, they are not quite as good with wheelchairs. So I have those welded in Sweden."

Despite his company name, Vigand is now partly on his way to using magnesium as a frame material. Titanium is usually described as a "forgiving" metal that has better vibration dampening properties than steel, but - according to Vigand - magnesium is even better.

"Because I'm lying down, with my head resting on the extended seat, any vibration goes straight to my skull. I've found before that, by the end of a race, I'm having trouble with my vision. With a magnesium frame, that doesn't happen."

The last thing Vigand does is to open a cardboard box and show off his new shoes, which look extremely strange.

"You see, they're angled so that the top of the foot continues in line with the leg. The design reduces air resistance considerably. They're the same shoes that bobsledders use."

HAND-BUILT BICYCLES have been having a renaissance lately. In England, there's an annual event for these bicycles, which aren't manufactured in an anonymous factory in Asia. The event, called Bespoked, is usually held in Bristol, but the year I visited the fair, it was held in London's Olympic Velodrome.

Just to have the opportunity to walk around Bespoked is a real treat for a cycle enthusiast. First, I encounter Louise from Brick Lane Bikes. I ask about their partnership with H&M, the international chain of clothing stores, about who came up with the idea for the partnership.

"It was H&M who came to us. We were the first company in London to build fixies, and H&M snatched them up. The collaboration resulted in a small range of cycling clothes and we built some bikes to stand in their shop windows around the world. We got a little PR and H&M found a new target group. The collection sold out straight away."

Then I get a lesson on titanium frames at Enigma's stand. On the walls they have beautiful pictures of southern England, Cornwall, where their factory is located. In one of the pictures, I spot Sean Yates, and I explain that I met him while cycling in Andalucía.

"We make all his bikes," says the Enigma guy. "Yates likes titanium; it was really popular when he was at the top of his game. He wore the yellow jersey in the Tour de France, of course. He won the Tour when he was the Team Sky manager. Nice guy, can talk for hours when he gets going."

"Well, in Andalucía he never got talking. I tried to start a conversation with him outside a house in Montecorto where we were both making use of the unprotected wifi. He barely replied."

"He can also be a little shy."

A fascinating man, anyway. Two heart attacks, a pacemaker and under constant suspicion of doping.

A bit further away, there are two guys who make a bicycle called a Bear. As a day job, they manufacture parts for aeroplanes and like working on projects that have a beginning and an end.

"What's special about your bicycle?"

"There's nothing special about it."

After that, I meet some Austrian frame builders.

"We meet every Wednesday in a basement and build frames and drink beer. It's mostly about drinking beer."

In their everyday lives, they're IT technicians, and they've developed a computer program to support other frame builders.

"Take a look at this," says the Austrian, showing me a bicycle frame on his laptop. "Here you enter your measurements, here you choose from all the tubes available on the market. A lot of pressure! And it shows you how the frame will look. Anyone who wants to can download it from the site. Ten thousand people have already downloaded it."

He had built a velodrome bike himself, which is extremely beautiful in a rough, industrial way.

"I wrapped it in linen cloths which I had soaked in saltwater. It turned out like this. After that, I just oiled it. I can only ride it indoors."

Following that, I speak with a man who makes really beautiful wooden wheels. Next, I have my behind measured by a saddle maker, admire De Rosa's bikes (even if they just don't feel handbuilt), talk to a guy from American Winter who looks more like a motorcyclist, squeeze into some cool leather shoes from Quoc Pham that would really suit a café racer and check out a bike brand called Sven.

It's at about this point that I decide I need to visit some of these enthusiastic yet commercial-minded manufacturers of handmade bikes in their own environment. I begin to look around at my options and book a few meetings, and then I start planning my tour.

SWALLOW BICYCLES The tiny Swallow bicycle workshop in Coalport is picturesque, as many things are in England. The River Severn meanders through the valley nearby, the brick buildings are old and worn and many are still coated in black, from the days when dense coal smoke polluted the air here. The air then was polluted with smoke because this was where the industrial revolution began. It was here that, for the first time, about two hundred and fifty years ago, people finally managed to cast steel. This was the prerequisite for making steel bridges, wheels, rails, steam boats, locomotives, steam cylinders and eventually bicycles.

Today there are eight museums and attractions related to this "steel age". Most famous is The Ironbridge, which symbolizes the whole era.

I arrive by bus, get off at the bridge and walk along the canal – the motorway of its day – passing many locks, until I reach Swallow's bicycle shop and factory.

Peter Bird is busy when I arrive and colleague Robert Wade isn't there. Just behind me, an older man jogs into the store. He's picking up his bike that was being serviced. He has been jogging through the woods for a few miles to get here and he's a bit impatient.

"Easter begins tomorrow, you know. We are having an 'open garden'. People pay a few quid to have a look around different private gardens and talk about flowers, garden architecture, landscaping. And drink tea, of course. Today I'm hoping to find the time to tidy our garden. I am a country doctor. I cycle to visit all my patients."

Peter brings out the doctor's bike, urging him to come back in a couple of weeks to get some new spokes, after which he pedals away along the canal like a scene from *Midsomer Murders*.

"We started 30 years ago," says Peter as he shows me around the small workshop. "Robert and I. We took a break for a few years when everyone, absolutely everyone, bought bikes made in Asia. But now it's better. Now we can feed our families again so we've restarted the business."

Peter shows me a tube, how to put on lugs and fit the bottom bracket, tighten it in his special, rather modern frame jig, where all the customers' dimensions can be fine-tuned. Next it's time to get the brass rod and start brazing.

"It gets hot when you're constructing a frame," says Peter. "Amateurs tend to use a thicker tube than is actually required, nervous that they might burn through their precious investment. I understand how you might think that, but for me, I try to be careful round the edges. It's about the colour of the hot metal. If you understand that, you don't make those kinds of mistakes."

Peter rummages briefly through a scrap box, finds an off-cut of tube, clamps it into a vice. Then he starts the blowtorch.

"Look: first, it will turn red, then orange and then yellow. Finally, the heat turns the tube white. Then it's too late. It's become a hole. The tube is ruined. But if you're careful and vigilant, it's no problem."

In 1993, Peter was the first in Britain to offer a frame-building course, a course he still teaches today. First, the participants come here and get their measurements taken. They browse through directories to choose the right tubes for the frame. A total of eleven pieces: three frame tubes, two front forks, two seat stays, two chain stays, a head tube and a steerer tube. Additionally, the bottom bracket casing, front and rear dropouts, and usually also two cross braces between the chain stays and between the seat stays. Then the lugs – plain or patterned – are chosen. Everything is picked according to personal taste, plus different attachment points for mudguards and racks if desired. Once all the parts have arrived, they come again for an intensive five-day course where the participants build their bikes together.

We come to a small showroom where there are actually some bikes for sale, although most of their frames are made to order and disappear as soon as they're ready. Some racers, a tourer and a couple of tandems gleam in the sunshine pouring through the old windows with their cast iron bars.

"When people stopped buying steel bikes," Peter recalls, "it was because they assumed that aluminium was so much lighter. The difference is actually quite small. Take Reynolds' finest frame, the 753. It's so thin, you can squash it with your fingers. But steel sounded heavy and aluminium sounded light. The truth is that it's industrially much easier to build an aluminium frame. It was the manufacturers who wanted the cyclists to change materials. Then came carbon fibre, which is even cheaper to manufacture. It's actually just plastic."

While Peter is talking, he points out some of the cheaper bicycles in the showroom. And now he says, almost with displeasure in his voice:

"Nowadays, we also sell bikes with aluminium and carbon fibre frames. But everything we manufacture ourselves is made of steel."

Today, there's a waiting list for those wishing to buy or build a Swallow frame. Eight weeks' wait time. At the London Fair, most of next year's production had already been reserved by interested cyclists with a lot of money in their pockets.

"Sure, it's a lot of money, but you can view it as an investment. We've only had one customer who ever came back and needed to buy another bike. And that was after 20 years."

FAGGIN I'm walking out of the centre of the Italian town of Padua. Beautiful mediaeval arcades, small shops, cafés and an astonishing number of places selling Catholic merchandise: Jesus on a cross, sacred figures, rosaries, baptismal fonts, clothes for priests and nuns. Who buys these, I wonder.

Many people are riding typical student bicycles, the sort of thing you buy when you arrive in a new city and find a used bike, hoping not to have to spend money on it more than once while you're there. You can identify such bikes by their tatty appearance, by the way they rattle and by the fact that, in many cases, they appear to be older than their riders.

Faggin is located on a small street of villas where some garden sheds have been converted into workshops of sorts. A small and unpromising yellow sign advertises "Hand-built Italian bikes." I find the door and peek into an empty workshop: a welder, a lathe, a stand which holds a bicycle frame. I knock. Out of the open window one floor above a woman leans out and says something in Italian. I only understand a single word, *aspetta*, "wait". So I wait.

Then Davide opens the door and invites me in to meet his father Massimo, mama Cristina (the woman in the window) and Alessandra, who works in the office. We take a tour of the small workshop, no bigger than a large garage. Massimo speaks. Davide translates. We look at a frame hanging from the ceiling.

"A prototype. To go on show at the Bespoke Fair in Bristol, England."

"The tubes are quite chunky," I say.

"Oversized," says Massimo, who turns out to understand and speak a little English.

All bicycles that are being built here are now tailor made. People come here, get measured, choose their own tubes, lugs and the model they want.

"Do people know what they want? Do they know their own measurements, the geometry of a frame, the features of a bicycle?"

"There are two types," explains Massimo. "The buyer of a tourer knows everything in advance. Exactly what tubes they want, the geometry, which fittings and what position they want to sit in. Then there are the others, often those who want a fixie. I hold up a tube and they say, 'That's great'. I show them a frame, they say, 'That's fine'. A fork, handlebars, wheels, it's always the same. But when it comes to the colour, they usually have an opinion."

"How many do you make?"

"Now we make 70 a year," says Massimo with a little sigh. "In the past, our all-time record was 351 in a single month."

"But not here?" I wondered.

"Well, there were 13 of us who worked here then. Three people brazing frames eight hours a day."

"Including my mother and her sister," Davide fills in.

Cristina goes and retrieves an old magazine which contains an entire article about her; an Italian woman building bicycle frames wasn't your average story back then.

A friend of the family comes in. A Faggin tourer is rolled into the front of the workshop. It has one of the best-known names in the cycling world: Tornosubito or "be back soon". This prototype was built for the friend because he was testing the model this summer.

The man begins a detailed story of exactly which roads he cycled, where he swung left and right, which lakes he passed and which mountains he climbed on his Tornosubito.

"I did 87km in 4 days," he says proudly, which doesn't really impress. "The test went well. My back was fine, my legs didn't take a beating. The geometry is perfect."

The family Faggin agrees with the friend's judgment.

I've always wondered what a bicycle builder does when a new model is being developed. Does he choose the tubes, build a frame, assemble a bike, test it, and then, if the worst comes to worst, do it all over again? It turns out that's exactly how it goes.

Massimo brings out a carbon fibre frame he built. It's beautiful, too. With extraordinary craftsmanship behind it. Massimo gives me a rather detailed account of how he built the moulds, chose the carbon fibre, how many fibres per square centimetre are best, how to arrange the different layers and always keep the material cold. He opens a freezer and points to a few sheets.

"Minus 18° celsius."

"What's the hardest thing to build: a steel frame or a carbon fibre one?" I wonder, thinking primarily about the process itself.

"Carbon fibre," replies Massimo, but he's not really talking about the process, more about the feeling afterwards. "When you braze or weld together a frame, you can see how the heat changes the colour of the metal. You are in charge of quality control. When you turn off the gas, you know if the joint is perfect. That is not the case with carbon fibre. It may have formed a small air bubble, the parts may not have been lined up exactly right, there may be a blemish in the epoxy that glues everything together. It is impossible to know with a carbon fibre frame. You can correct a steel frame if it has become a bit wonky."

It's obvious that, although Faggin's carbon fibre frame is exquisitely crafted, carbon fibre is not something he wants to devote himself to. He only does it to make sure that the business doesn't go under.

Then we go and get coffee. I'm shown an exquisite green frame Massimo built for himself. At the moment he's building one more for L'Eroica, the annual vintage race in Chianti. On the wall is a photo of the Italian national cycling team at the Olympic Games in 1984. They rode Faggin bikes.

"Although we didn't get our logo on the frame. You didn't get that back then."

"How did the Olympic race go?"

"I don't remember."

We drink coffee and eat Cristina's apple pie. On my tablet I show them a listing for a 1980s Faggin bike for sale online. The family thinks it's a good price. Nowadays, collectors really value those bikes.

The coffee break continues for a while. It's quiet in the workshop. Nearly all orders are placed in the spring. As if customers have a sense of planning ahead.

"Though we are building some for the Australian market. It's spring there now. Faggin can actually be found all over the world. They are sold in Taiwan and in Chile. A female cycle courier in Los Angeles has three. She came here to join us and build the third," concludes Massimo, pointing to a faded photo of the family and a big blonde woman with small braids in her hair, tacked to a bulletin board under an advertisement for pizza delivery.

JAEGHER At Jaegher, Belgian Diel Vaneenooghe is sitting grinding a welded joint when I arrive at the workshop. Being extremely careful, he smooths the surface with a rotating tool that sends shivers up my spine with unpleasant memories.

"Sounds like a dentist's drill," I say when Diel turns off the machine.

"It does. Makes seven thousand revolutions per minute."

Jaegher has a reputation for cool. Their models are often seen in trendy magazines and on blogs that showcase only the most beautiful and stylish bikes. They've managed to build a brand because they know what lies at the heart of a brand: stories.

Diel offers me coffee and shows me a newspaper cutting from this summer. It's about the Transcontinental endurance race, which started in London and finished in Istanbul. No support. The clock is running the whole time. A huge distance and some of it over parts of the Alps.

"Do you see this?" says Diel, pointing to the cutting. "A total of 11 countries. They rode 3,363km (2,090 miles) in 7 days and 23 hours. And won on a Jaegher!"

"Was it good for sales?"

"Extremely good. The phone was ringing off the hook the next day."

Three years ago, the factory was at a crossroads. Previously, the most popular frames had been made elsewhere for others who simply put their brand name on the bikes before selling them. But that was no longer financially lucrative.

"How long have you been around?"

"For four generations."

"In the same building?"

"No no! My grandfather was on the other side of the road."

His answers are short and abrupt, like little barks. You have to tease the words out of him. So, three years ago, when faced with the reality of having to make even cheaper bicycles to survive, instead they chose to invest in a premium brand. Quality bicycles. Expensive. Only for those who could afford them.

"Now I only build with the best tubes from Columbus. Reynolds makes an equally good product, but I had problems with their deliveries."

Nowadays, Diel sells his bikes exclusively with Campagnolo components. Columbus and Campagnolo, a completely Italian bike built in Belgium.

"No titanium bikes?" I wonder.

"No. Why should I build in titanium? I would have to increase the thickness of the tubes to a millimetre. Now I use 0.45mm."

I don't really understand why the thickness of the tube would matter if the quality is better. You can still maintain the slim size of steel; you don't have to go all the way up to the overblown size of an aluminium tube. Diel goes to get a Columbus stainless steel tube to show me. The tubes are uncomfortably thin and do not feel very substantial.

"How long does it take you to build a frame?"

"Ten hours."

I'm trying to understand what goes into the cost of a frame. Is it the material? Not really; the parts aren't very expensive. Is it time and labour? To some extent, although it's not as if Diel has spent months carving a mahogany chest of drawers.

"Some painters only take four hours to do a painting," Diel says as if he understood what I was thinking.

The cost is actually a combination of factors. If you buy a Jaegher, or any other handmade bike, you know that a professional chose the parts, a professional built the frame, a professional fitted the bike with top components. If you have the money, you don't have to think about more than simply choosing the right brand. The price of a finished Jaegher is also a reminder of what craftmanship costs. In the early days of the bicycle, a good bike cost as much as an annual salary for a worker. Today, you can get away with just a week's wages for a good bike. These cheaper prices say something about how much is saved when production is mechanized, but also about how little money the workers manufacturing bikes in Asia earn. But if you want a hand-built bicycle crafted by a professional you still have to pay for it, even today.

"We're already selling all over the world," says Diel, changing the subject.

"Do customers come here and get their measurements taken?"

"No, no, they can do it all on our website. They can put in their dimensions, choose the model and the colour. Then we build and send out the bikes. We have customers in China and Switzerland, the United States and Singapore."

"Singapore? It's an island, only a few miles wide."

"Not my problem," says Diel, shrugging his shoulders. "By the way, the guy in Singapore has already bought two. He's one of my best customers."

On the wall behind Diel hangs a canary yellow bicycle with the logo of Cohiba on it, the cigar manufacturer. There is a chapter elsewhere in this book about all the different frame builders in Belgium – that they value the good things in life, don't care about cycling communities and their healthy trends, smoke expensive cigars and build expensive bicycles. These things can make you a success in some circles. The stories that build brands. The way legends often do.

"My grandfather," Diel says, in one of his few talkative moments, "was a pretty good racing cyclist. But then World War II and the Germans came. They went from house to house and collected metal to melt down into bullets, grenades and bombs.

Grandfather did not want to get rid of his bike so took it to pieces, oiled all the parts and packed them into a big cloth bag, which he hid in a hole in the ground right here." Diel waves his arm toward the window. Outside, I can see a tractor ploughing a muddy field. "After the war, Grandpa dug up his bike. We still have it somewhere."

DARIO PEGORETTI is perhaps the most mythologized frame builder still operating. Pegoretti hides from the world up in the little northern Italian town of Caldonazzo, grants few interviews, has a website that is largely unfinished, rarely answers emails (at least not to my interview request) and has a bad reputation when it comes to deliveries.

Nevertheless, it was Pegoretti who built the last steel frame to win the Tour de France, the one that Miguel Indurain rode in 1994, even though it had Pinarello's logo on the frame. Pegoretti's trick was said to have been lowering the rear end of the top tube by a centimetre. Myth? Probably.

Pegoretti has moved on from creating magically innovative steel frames, to also making them beautifully extravagant. He gives them names like Big Leg Emma, after a song by Frank Zappa, and paints them afterwards, while others have names like So What, Wild, or Ayers Rock.

When American actor Robin Williams died, people learned that he was a big cycling enthusiast and that he had a bicycle collection worth about as much as Jay Leno's cars. He also had a special favourite, one that he always rode, a Pegoretti. So when it was time for the 2008 North American Handmade Bicycle Show, and word got around that Dario Pegoretti would attend, Robin Williams climbed aboard his private jet and flew to Portland to attend. After that visit, Williams, Pegoretti and some industry people went out for dinner. It's said that the dinner was long and fun, but also serious because Pegoretti had just recovered from cancer. The evening is said to have concluded with the stand-up comedian doing a spot-on impression of the hippified, eccentric Italian frame builder.

Once, on impulse, I bought a Pegoretti online. I've never regretted it. Every time I see it, it makes me happy. The model is a Marcelo, a red one. Sometimes I wish it was the more artistic model Marcelo Thelonius, named after the musician Thelonius Monk, and therefore decorated with notes in jazz blue tones.

Being a Swede, I wonder if there are any Swedish frame builders? Not many, I think, apart from the adventurous die-hards who build their own frames in their garages at home. However, I find two frames at a bicycle fair in Stockholm.

Patrik Tegnér and Mikael Przysuski have a small stand dominated by Tegnér's very beautiful tourer, every detail of which has been designed without reference to the usual conventions of frame-building. Even the saddle – it isn't a Brooks, which is usually what people choose if they want to sit on leather.

"No, it's a Gilles Berthoud," says Patrik when I ask. "French. They do some other things, as well. Saddle bags and panniers and so on."

A little while later, a man comes up to Mikael and asks if he could build a frame from an old set of tubes he has in the attic. The man looks more like an old rock and roll singer than a cyclist.

"Why do you have a set of tubes in your attic?" wondered Mikael, puzzled.

"It was first prize in a cycling competition in England. I won it. In the 1970s. I remember that those were the best tubes around. Reynolds or something."

"I can certainly build a frame using your set of tubes," Mikael says, still a bit confused by the request, and gives the old rocker his business card.

"A really weird prize. A set of tubes," I say.

"But he must have been a really good cyclist, if he won a race in England."

THE HAUTE ROUTE consists of three cycling events, to which anyone can subscribe, with the common theme of "one week of cycling in mountainous terrain". Advertised under the byline "Ride Like a Pro", the events are marketed as being suitable for everyone – from rookie to expert – but as a beginner, I wouldn't attempt such a race until I'd at least tried riding up a mountain. Because, unless you live in seriously mountainous terrain, you can cycle a whole lifetime without realizing quite what a long, steep climb means, and without understanding that a mountain is not just a really big hill.

At the time of writing this book, the event races are: Haute Route Dolomites–Swiss Alps (from Geneva to Venice), the Haute Route Pyrénées (from the Basque Coast to Barcelona) and the

Haute Route Alps (from Geneva to Nice). Tragically, the latter event gained notoriety outside the cycling world in 2012 when the journalist and entrepreneur Pontus Schultz died in an accident on the way down Gorges du Cyan, in a ravine just above the finish line in Nice.

For the most part, the Haute Route is organized by a profit-making company called OC Sport. There are several others who organize similar cycling adventures where you ride a bicycle and your luggage follows behind in the support vehicle. Uber-trendy Rapha Cycle Club in London organizes smaller, more exclusive trips, and includes one route across the Pyrenees, which begins in French Biarritz on the Atlantic coast and ends in Collioure on the Mediterranean. Thomson Bike Tours offer a week's cycling through Portugal, the Trans Portugal Challenge, covering a distance of 822km (511 miles). You can find a host of others online.

THE HEALTH BENEFITS of cycling are numerous, there's no doubt about that. The greatest benefits, of course, are for people who replace a sedentary activity with an activity on two wheels. For example, those who leave their car in the garage and start cycling to work. But the list goes on. Here are some of the stats. A cyclist:

➺ loses on average 7kg (15lb) in their first year as a commuter
➺ who is a woman and starts cycling 30km (19 miles) a week reduces her risk of cardiovascular disease by 50 percent
➺ has lower blood pressure
➺ has a better balance between good and bad cholesterol
➺ has a reduced risk of Type 2 diabetes
➺ doesn't get as easily worried or stressed
➺ has increased muscle strength, not least the abdominal muscles, which can lead to reduced back problems
➺ lives longer
➺ takes half as many sick days
➺ sleeps better
➺ has better coordination
➺ has a stronger immune system
➺ has better digestion
➺ has better memory
➺ has a better chance of getting pregnant and an easier pregnancy

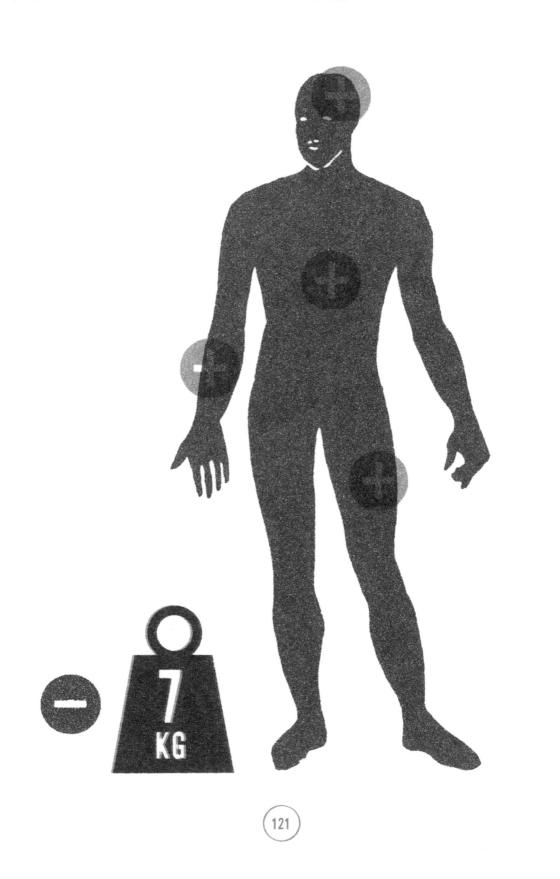

➤➤ has a better sex life, with the biggest difference being for men over 50 who cycle more than three hours a week
➤➤ has a reduced risk of certain types of cancer
➤➤ has a reduced risk of dementia and Alzheimer's

Improving health through exercise isn't exactly news. In ancient times, the Roman author Juvenal coined the phrase *Mens sana in corpore sano* or "a healthy mind in a healthy body". Nevertheless, new findings are constantly reinforcing this idea. Such as discovering that exercise may encourage the production of new brain cells. So you can ride your way to a bigger brain.

Other new findings suggest reasons why cyclists have a greater chance of staying healthy and living longer. It may be partly due to the fact that people who exercise have longer telomeres. The telomeres are the caps on the ends of strings of DNA that protect the chromosomes against damage. People with longer telomeres are better able to avoid the damage that occurs constantly in the strands of DNA and have a better chance of avoiding the formation of tumors. The length of our telomeres is linked to our biological age, not our chronological age. So the longer the telomeres, the "younger" our bodies are.

Another fairly new study reveals that short, daily, low-intensity exercise is better for your health than longer periods of intense exercise a couple of times a week. It's sitting still that's unhealthy. This is true even of a person who is slightly overweight but who walks to and from work. This slightly overweight person will live longer than a skinny person who commutes by car. Being skinny is a beauty ideal, not a measure of health. An overweight person who walks for 2½ hours a week lives an average of 3.1 years longer than a person of normal weight who is primarily sedentary. These results come from a recent study of six hundred and fifty thousand people over forty years.

The study could just as equally be all about cyclists, and for most of the points in the list above, you can exchange a bicycle for another form of daily exercise. The bicycle isn't a miracle machine – but it's perfect for getting daily exercise to and from work, especially in comparison with the driver who has to go back out to the gym after they come home in the evening.

In addition, some forms of exercise, such as exercising indoors in a gym, might not be as beneficial as cycling. Firstly, exercising in the sunshine is more effective than an equal effort indoors. Studies have shown that exercise in daylight leads to better results in terms of body composition, that is, the balance between muscles, fat and bone. Cycling under a blue sky decreases fat and increases muscle mass far more effectively than spinning in a gym. Exercising in an enriching environment also increases the formation of brain cells. Outdoor activities where all of our senses – sight, hearing, taste, smell, touch – are stimulated is perhaps the best thing we can do to help new brain cells develop.

Jogging in the forest has all the positive effects of a good bike ride. Furthermore, jogging is more efficient than cycling, regardless of whether you are comparing time or distance covered. But jogging is also much more demanding on your body. It's more punishing to jog than to cycle. This applies even more the older or heavier you are. One of the really nice things about cycling is that even if you're unfit, advancing in years, or carrying love handles, you can, in principle, pedal without hurting yourself, even when you are performing at your max. As a cyclist, you can simply achieve a greater amount of exercise before you begin to have problems with inflammation and aching or injured muscles and joints.

THE HELMET is something I started wearing for cycling late in life and only after my father died. His last words were: "Johan, be careful!" His words surprised and annoyed me and still do to this day. It was surprising because he'd never said anything like that to me before – not when I was hitchhiking across Europe, or when I travelled to China before it was truly open to tourists, or when I bought a motorcycle. I was irritated because I would rather have got some advice that helped me realize the true values of life: quit your job, travel the world, have ten children, at least.

"Be careful."

So the day after my father died, I went and bought a cycle helmet. It was my first cycle helmet. I was 44 years old. Apart from that, I decided to live as carelessly as I had before.

The fact that I hadn't previously worn a helmet was really a generational thing. I belong to the last generation who "escaped" wearing a helmet while cycling – partly as a matter of attitude. Cycling was associated with freedom and beauty and environmentally friendly transport, whereas a helmet was an

order from the State. Sure, it was dangerous to crash a car, but then cars drove too fast and should be slower. Cyclists shouldn't have to wear safety equipment to venture out onto the roads. Requiring the use of a helmet might lead to fewer bicycles and more cars.

When I talked to cyclists in countries such as Holland, Belgium and England, many of them seem almost perplexed when I discuss helmets. They say it's a non-issue. They say that if you got rid of cars, helmets would be unnecessary. They say making helmets a legal requirement might put people off riding bicycles.

I'm reading British statistics on road accidents involving cyclists not wearing helmets. If the car is travelling at 20mph (32kph), 97 percent of cyclists survive; at 35mph (56kph), 50 percent of cyclists die; and at 50mph (80kph), 99 percent of cyclists die. There aren't any statistics regarding the cyclists' speed, so I suppose that must be a combined speed. The interesting thing about the survey isn't the exact speeds involved, but how quickly it escalates from basically harmless to fully life-threatening. This fact is used by those who hate helmets to show that if we could only ride on roads without cars, there would be no danger. But it's also used by helmet advocates to say that a crash at 50mph (80kph) with a helmet is like a crash without one at 20mph (32kph) – you probably survive. Then the helmet-haters say that most fatalities happen when swerving trucks and buses crush cyclists, and there's no helmet in the world that would have saved them. Helmet advocates claim that 80 percent of all bicycle accidents involve the cyclist alone, often caused by insufficiently swept cycle lanes and poor cycle lane crossings, and they cite the fact that features in cycle lanes are often made from steel, concrete and glass. When a cyclist crashes against them, helmets save lives and protect against permanent brain damage.

After 11 years of cycling with a helmet, I no longer think about this ugly-looking Styrofoam bowl on my head. But, it should be acknowledged, I've also reached the age where I no longer care about what I look like when I ride a bike. I've reached the age when I go to shops with my cycle clips still around the bottoms of my trousers (but I'm not so old that I keep my helmet on while I'm shopping).

At the bicycle museum in the Flemish city of Roeselare, I stroll around and look at the wide range of old-fashioned tricycles for women who had to wear long skirts, and the track bicycles from 1910, which look like fixies from 2010. Then I reach an exhibit that, at first glance, looks like an uninteresting set of memorabilia from a successful athlete: some cups, some sports gear, some newspaper cuttings from his career. But then I realize that the bike in the display has been crashed and the newspaper shows a man lying on the tarmac looking mortally wounded.

"Is he dead?" I ask Thomas Ameye, my guide.

"Yes, he's dead. Jempi Monseré was his name. He was cycling in the peloton. He wasn't looking, and when he broke away from the others, he rode into a stationary car. Killed instantly."

I look at the article again. The car can be seen in the background of the photo. The entire front window is smashed and it looks like a moose accident. Showing on a television next to the newspaper is footage of the 1970 Road World Championships in Leicester and a very young Jean-Pierre 'Jempi' Monseré is winning gold. Monseré has a bright future ahead of him. A year later, he's dead. His career ended abruptly with an encounter with a Mercedes at about 30mph (48kph).

It would take 20 years before the UCI (Union Cycliste Internationale) took up the helmet issue and in 1991, at the Paris–Nice competition, demanded that cyclists wear head gear. The result? The cyclists went on strike and the UCI backed down from their demands.

The helmet only became obligatory in competitions in 2003, a few weeks after the top Kazak cyclist Andrej Kivilev died in a crash. Initially, however, there were a lot of exceptions. For example, you were allowed to ride without a helmet for the last 5km (3 miles) of a mountain stage.

"But isn't it a little macabre to show a picture of a dead person like this, the picture in the newspaper and his things in the museum?" I wonder.

"Well, a little bit. But we had a discussion with his family. They live here in town. They wanted this." Then Thomas Ameye pauses rather dramatically, deciding whether to say more or to leave it at that. But then he decides to continue. "A few years after his death, Jempi's little son rode out in the road on his bike and was hit by a car. He died too. It is said that he was wearing a copy of his dad's world champion shirt, but I don't know. It sounds a bit like an urban myth."

I don't ask if the son was wearing a helmet.

HIPSTER The 'Hipster Factory', also known as Shinola, is located in Detroit. I happen to be passing the factory and turn off Lincoln Highway to head north toward Detroit. This city, more than any other, is associated with the automotive industry and, lately, an automotive industry in deep decline. I'm here because I saw a documentary called *Bike Culture in Detroit*. Shortly after the turn of the millennium, Detroit's problems began. By 2010, the city had lost 25 percent of its population and on 18 July 2013, it filed for bankruptcy. The documentary suggested that after the city had hit rock bottom, it was possible to rebuild it with the bicycle as the shining star. If for no other reason than out of necessity. People without work couldn't afford a car and a city with an economy in free fall can't afford to provide public transport. Only the bike is left standing. In the documentary, they interviewed some people who make bicycles, others who run a so-called bicycle kitchen where children could get a bicycle for free, and people who organize a critical mass of cyclists every Monday to take part in a slow roll, where thousands of cyclists gather to cycle slowly through the city.

About eight miles before I reach Detroit, the state of the road deteriorates and for the rest of the journey, I bump along in my rental car. It's clear that the money has already run out before I see the first abandoned skyscraper, the first house with boarded windows, the first industrial complex that stopped producing anything, and the first deserted car park. One should be careful about making comparisons with war, which is obviously much worse. But the city of Detroit gives the impression of having been bombed, with whole neighborhoods abandoned in among the areas where there's still some activity and where people still live.

I stop outside Shinola, enter their shop and immediately think this is a hipster factory. There are watches, leather accessories, pet accessories and, of course, bicycles. Like a gourmet restaurant where you can watch a chef's elegant dance in front of the stove through a glass window, you can see tattooed, bearded young men screwing together a Runwell or a Bixby.

I consider Shinola to be a hipster factory because they attach so much importance to the stories behind their products. This is made evident by the difficulty I encounter just trying to get to speak to someone in charge. Everybody is friendly but stress that it's extremely important that I speak to the right person. They liaise with their California communications office and their marketing department and their communications-whatever, and finally I want to shout: "You make bikes, and you're not the first in the world to do so!" But I decide against it.

My most recent email conversation I have with Shinola reads:

"But there won't be anyone who can show you how the bikes are assembled."

"That doesn't matter. I'll bring my own screwdriver and see if I can do it myself." A comment their senior account manager thought was pretty funny.

It's Saturday morning when I step into Shinola's shop/factory/workshop. The premises are very nice: scrubbed tile facade on a building that has been a small factory of some kind, huge windows in cast-iron frames, all the products are displayed on tables, image-boosting lifestyle magazines are scattered about, one of which is called *Lula* and has Lykke Li on the cover.

I grab a salesperson and ask him to tell me about Shinola. I see how he hesitates, trained as he is to refer any press enquiries to California, but it's Saturday so he'll have to do the talking.

He says that Shinola was originally a brand of shoe polish, well known and steeped in tradition.

"Linking it with Detroit gave it even more weight. 'Shinola Detroit' breathes American quality."

I nod at the little bottles of shoe polish that Mark points to, while he explains that there's something about the brand that still makes them sell.

"Watches. It was a watch that we first started to manufacture," Mark continues, showing some elegant watches.

And then it becomes clear why they're so careful about their dealings with the press, and so careful about which stories are told because those are what sell their products. In terms of performance, one can easily find an equally good, but much cheaper watch from Asia. But this is Shinola in Detroit and price tags start at $550.

It's the same thing with the bikes. Mark picks up a Runwell with a bright red steel frame and a front carrying rack.

"The front is designed like a French *porteur*," says Mark, "like they used to ride to deliver newspapers in Paris."

This adds another layer to Shinola's story: Parisian newspaper delivery riders.

"The saddles we manufacture ourselves, but not the frame. That's made by Schwinn, but here in the United States. Take a look. See how nicely made it is."

And it definitely is a nice bike. It's a beautiful bike. But I understand Mark's emphasis on "here in the US" because it's no longer obvious. The highly affluent Chicago company Schwinn started manufacturing bicycles in 1895 and a hundred years later, they were the market leaders in the United States. But then they missed the BMX trend as well as the trend for easier racing bikes and mountain bikes. In 2001, Schwinn went bankrupt, was sold and after a few years all bicycles labelled Schwinn were made in China.

"All of them, and at least 99 percent of the bikes sold in the US are now manufactured in China," says Mark with a gloomy sigh. "But now we're on the way back. Schwinn too."

"Do you have a Shinola yourself?"

"No, God, I can't afford that," Mark replied, blushing easily.

I'm ashamed of my question because, in my haste, I forgot what a wretched salary people in the US service industry earn.

"But," I say, to change the subject, "isn't it strange that the Shinola is equipped with Japanese Shimano gears when you have American SRAM from Chicago a few miles away? Wouldn't that have been better for your brand? The all-American bike?"

"Yes," replied Mark, "I don't really understand why they chose Shimano."

I get back in my rental car and drive around Detroit in search of the new bicycle boom. There's a lot of people cycling, I have to admit, but to describe it as any kind of social movement would be wrong. Detroit is, of course, still a very spread-out city designed for drivers and it's not like all car manufacturing has ceased. There are still over ten thousand people here working for Chevrolet, Chrysler and other large US car manufacturers. And the number of deserted car parks doesn't make the city feel any smaller. There are quite long distances between everything and it's not realistic to say that people who can't afford a car would be able to travel those distances by bicycle. Though you never know. Something good might come from bankruptcy and relocation. The cyclists may hang their hopes on the city's motto: *Speramus meliora; Resurget cineribus* – which means something like "We hope for better things; It will rise from the ashes."

HOLIDAY CYCLING for training and exercise has become more common. Not only are the small specialist travel agencies offering advanced cycling holidays in places such as Tuscany or Mallorca, but the big charter companies now also run adventure cycling holidays to the Canary Islands or Turkey, for example.

The advantage of package travel is, of course, that you don't have to worry about the details, you just book, pay, travel and ride a bike. As a cyclist travelling abroad, it's easy to misunderstand what you are letting yourself in for. The first time I rode in Andalucía, we rode out of the village for no more than 5 minutes

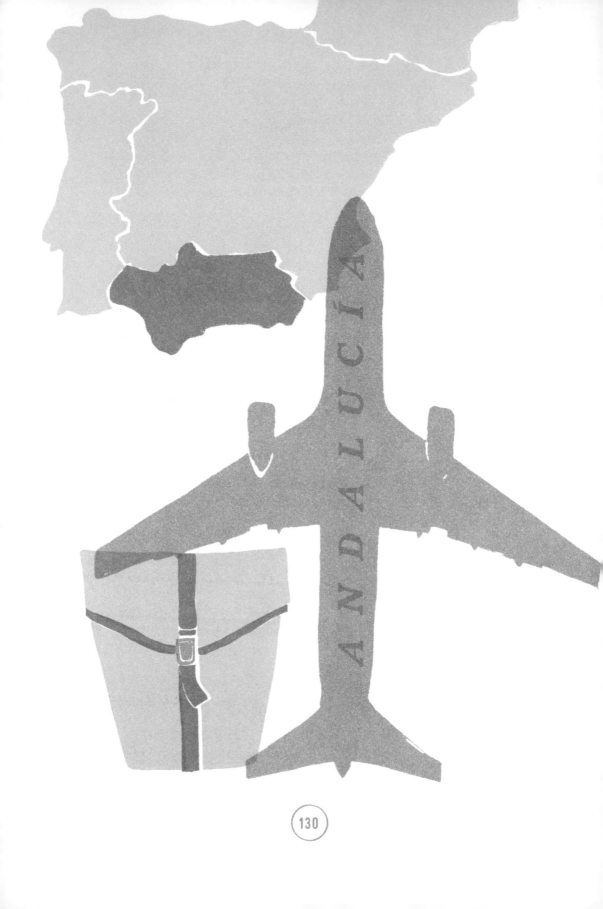

before our guide pointed to a hill and said, "Up we go! See you at the top – it's 7km (4½ miles)." A 7km uphill? He must be joking, I thought. But he wasn't. In Sweden, we measure the amount of exercise by the length of the ride, while in other places they measure it by the total ascent. After a week's mountain biking, I wanted new knee caps for Christmas.

So, don't just say to yourself, "I'm going to ride up the Alpe d'Huez on my holiday," without first checking what other cycling holidays might be available in that area. Using only two gears, the lowest up and the highest down, for a whole week will be exhausting. Check online before booking. There are lots of mapped routes, especially if you use Garmin or Strava GPS services, where you can check the distances and the altitude. You'll really feel 1,000m (3,280ft) of altitude in one day. Two thousand is tough, and three thousand and above are only for the really fit.

Another thing to consider is the climate. It's easy to choose a climate that's too hot. Certainly, 30°C (86°F) is fine if you are lying by the pool, but maybe not what you're looking for while in the saddle. Some destinations have realized this, like Mallorca, where they start the season earlier and continue later because cyclists want it a bit cooler than most holidaymakers. Andalucía is an excellent cycling destination in the winter, with daytime temperatures of 15-20°C (59-68°F), quite cheap flights to Málaga, and a wealth of good-value lodging options to choose from. Lots of cyclists go there so they can get pedalling while the snow still prevents them exercising at home. Other destinations, like Corsica, have yet to understand this. If you arrive at the end of April, when the island is at its most beautiful and there are fewer cars on the road, half of all hotels and restaurants are closed and you'll be lucky if you can force the bicycle rental man out of his winter sleep to reluctantly pump up the tyres and knock the spiderwebs off a bike.

Also, it's worth finding out the population density in the area you are planning to visit, and the extent of good tarmac roads. My favourite island, Sicily, isn't really ideal for cycling simply because there are five million people living there. Corsica is even more crowded. However, even though Mallorca is even more densely populated than the other two islands, there they've realized the usefulness of building cycle tracks.

If you're travelling independently and want to hire a bike, the first thing that you need to find is a good bicycle hire place, of which there are fewer around than you might think. Certainly, there are some in those places where cycling holidays are commonplace, but apart from these, it can be more difficult to find one. Of course, the best thing to do is search the web. In Ronda in Andalucía (fly to Málaga) there is a really good bicycle hire. Other examples would be around Mont Ventoux (fly to Marseilles) in the provinces of Bédoin and Malaucène, as well as in the many cities in the Friuli region of northern Italy (fly to Venice or Treviso).

Whether you bring your own bike or rent one when you arrive is a matter of personal taste. Personally, I hardly think it's worthwhile to put up with all the effort of bringing your own bike just for a week's cycling. If you're training for a race, it's good to get used to your own bike, but it's not that big a difference. The important thing is that you're sitting on a bicycle, not whose bicycle it is. If you choose to bring your own bike, there are further things to consider.

Airlines. Most airlines charge an additional fee, usually calculated by distance. And if you come with a bicycle bag, you have to consider transport from the airport. If you hire a car, it will have to be a fairly big one, which may seem unnecessary because you'll be leaving the car all day every day when you're off cycling. Of course, there's also the matter of whether you want to cycle with others or prefer to ride solo. If I don't have friends with me, I prefer the latter.

As I write this, I'm sitting in Álora, Andalucía, in a very large rental house. I took a commuter train from Málaga airport and a shuttle bus from the train station to Álora, which is situated on top of a hill. From the airport to my rented house it took less than an hour and it was easy to bring my bike bag with me on both rail and bus. Álora is small and it only takes a few minutes to get out of town on my bike, but it's still big enough that there are two bicycle shops here and a bicycle hire in the neighbouring village. I've just returned from a 60km (37 mile) ride with a total ascent of 1,200m (3,937ft) during which I didn't encounter more than 20 cars. It's a sunny day, and around 20°C (68°F). It's also the middle of January.

HORIZONTAL PARKING is a playful term for the cyclist who topples over, either at a slow speed or while standing still. Most often, during horizontal parking, the cyclist fails to free their cycle shoes from the pedals. Another term for horizontal parking is an SPD Fall, which derives from the most common system for locking cycle shoes into pedals, Shimano Pedalling Dynamics.

HORS CATÉGORIE is the French term for mountains that are extraordinarily difficult to ride up. The phrase means "outside the classification" and refers to a situation in which the usual system of classifying hills on a scale of 1–4, with 1 as the toughest, is just not sufficient.

In the early days, *Hors catégorie* was defined by any steep mountain pass that was impossible to climb in a car.

A HÖVDING is a brand of airbag for cyclists. It was designed by Anna Haupt and Terese Alstin in 2005 and forms a kind of stiff collar around your neck. An inflatable helmet then unfolds and covers the head upon impact, when the cyclist crashes or falls off the bike. Apparently, it offers better protection than an ordinary helmet, but is probably bought primarily by those who want to ride with the wind in their hair, or arrive at their destination without helmet hair.

HUNTING & CYCLING stores were, at one time, not considered an unusual combination. Being able to service a bicycle while offering advice on the right kind of gun cartridges was considered to be as obvious as a bicycle mechanic today serving a caffè macchiato made with fair-trade beans.

A HYBRID is a blend of bicycles. I bought myself one 24 years ago after my old bike was stolen. The thieves had broken a window at my workplace and taken all the computers and the bike that was in my office.

At the beginning of the 1990s, a hybrid was a fairly new phenomenon in bicycle circles. Its tyres were almost as thin as a racer, but it had more of the mountain bike's robust frame and straight handlebars. Actually, the mixture contained a third bike, the typical urban cycle, because my hybrid also had mudguards, racks, lighting and a dynamo.

In cycling circles, it's amusing to say that the number of bikes a cyclist needs can be determined by the formula n + 1, where n is the number of bikes the cyclist already has. Sometimes this is the number of bikes that one's partner accepts. However, there's always room for "just one more". But there's also the urge to find that cool bicycle that can be used for more than one thing. A two-in-one bike. Over the years, this type of bicycle has popped up under many different names. Some have been called "commuter bicycles" or "city racers". Even so, they've generally been slightly less well equipped than my hybrid.

Recently, a new term in the hybrid jungle appeared: "gravel", like a gravel path. These bikes first appeared in the American Midwest in Iowa, Kansas and Illinois, where you could ride quite a long amateur run over a wide range of different surfaces. On the whole, a gravel looks like a cycle cross bike but, as one salesman pointed out, it has different geometry, even though it's hard to see with the naked eye. The idea is that a cycle cross bike doesn't work as well as a hybrid because it's built for short, fast, bumpy tracks and therefore needs to be a quick-to-react, slightly nervous bike. A gravel, on the other hand, is built for longer rides, has a somewhat more upright position and generally resembles the older tourer, which has been around for a long time.

INBREEDING among people in the countryside disappeared when the bicycle became universally accessible. Or at least that's what some people claim. Instead of simply putting up with what was available, young women and men could ride miles away, to a city, a beach or a dance hall, to find a better partner.

THE INVENTIONS that, in my opinion, are the top 10 bicycle innovations (in no particular order) are:

1. THE CHAIN

The year is 1789. Englishman Henry J Lawson patents his chain-driven safety bicycle called the Bicyclette. The chain allows for a simpler and safer system for gearing than before, when the size of the wheel determined the speed. It was called a safety cycle because chain operation meant that the cyclist no longer needed to sit 2m (6ft 5in) up in the air to pedal.

2. BICYCLE TUBES

The Englishman RW Thompson invented the air-filled rubber wheel in 1845, but it took more than 40 years for this innovation to finally replace solid rubber tyres. In 1888, the Scotsman John Boyd Dunlop succeeded in commercializing Thompson's genius.

3. LED LIGHT

The LED light recently celebrated its fiftieth anniversary. But it's only in recent years that LED lights have begun emitting enough light and cost little enough to be practical for use on bicycles. Today, you can buy powerful LED lights powered by batteries or a dynamo.

Electric bicycle lighting arrived in 1888. The problems with these lights didn't change until LED lighting was introduced: they were either heavy and impractical with batteries, or they were powered by a dynamo that rarely stayed attached and often slipped when it was raining.

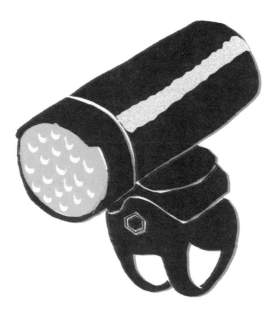

4. THE CLIPLESS PEDAL

In 1985, Bernard Hinault won the Tour de France with clipless pedals made by the French company Look. This was the moment the clipless pedal system really had its breakthrough, a system in which cycle shoes equipped with special cleats slot into the pedals, where they remain until the cyclist twists the foot to unlock them. Before Look's breakthrough development, the Italian company Cinelli, ten years earlier, had launched a system where the cyclist had to bend down and release a locking device by hand. Not surprisingly, this system became known as "suicide pedals".

The clipless pedal replaced an older tried-and-tested system in which a cyclist inserted his shoes into a little basket on the pedal. These can still be found on some café racers and fixies.

5. SATELLITE NAVIGATION

With a GPS (Global Positioning System) on the handlebars, a cyclist can choose and follow a downloaded route, find home again and then, connected to the internet, compare the trip with previous rides or with other riders.

Along the way, a GPS delivers all manner of statistics such as current speed, distance travelled so far, average speed, peak speed and total ascent, as well as distance cycled on downhill stretches.

A GPS can also perform other tasks unrelated to the satellites it's connected to, such as measuring pace, heart rate and ambient temperature.

6. GEARS

Being able to get up that really steep hill or achieve that really high speed wouldn't have been possible without gears. Manual gears are increasingly being replaced by electronic ones. In most cases, however, three is enough; especially if you live in Sweden like me, as it is a fairly flat country.

7. THE BALANCE BIKE

The balance bike, or run bike, is a great toy for young children who aren't quite ready for a pedal bike. A balance bike is quite similar to Baron Karl von Drais' "run machine" from 1817. Where was the balance bike when I was a kid?

8. COMBO LEVER

In 1990, Japanese company Shimano introduced the STI, Shimano Total Integration, a lever for both braking and changing gear. This makes gear changes faster and safer as the cyclist doesn't have to change hand position and fumble with the lever. A cyclist can also change gear while standing in the pedals.

9. SUSPENSION

In 1987, the American Paul Turner created a bicycle with both rear and front suspension and presented it at a bicycle industry trade show. Thus was born the predecessor for most of today's bikes built for off-road riding.

10. FOLDING BICYCLE

In 1878, the British inventor WHJ Grout patented his folding penny-farthing. It was more of a bicycle that could be disassembled and reassembled, rather than a bike that could be quickly folded up as you were running to catch the steam train.

In 1915, Bianchi made a folding bike for the Italian military, while in 1939, Frenchman AJ Marcelin introduced his "Le Petit Bi", a folding bike with a 16-inch wheel and a surprisingly modern design.

JOUR SANS is the French term for a day when a racing cyclist totally lacks any strength and energy. Literally, "a day without". In Italian, you usually say *giornata no*.

L

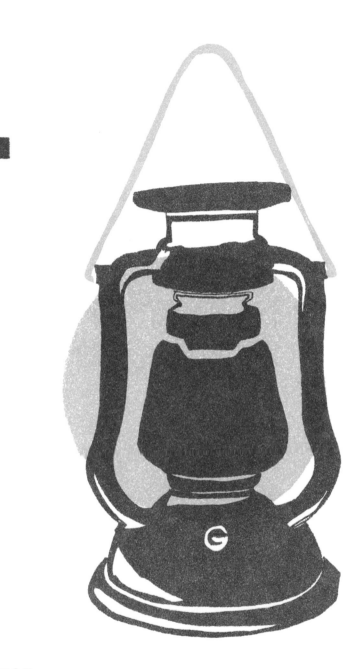

LANTERNE ROUGE is French for "red lantern" and refers to the light that used to hang on the back of the rear carriage of a train. It refers to the cyclist who finishes last, who sees the train driving away. In cycling, it's quite common that even the *lanterne rouge* in a race gets a prize.

LEADER'S JERSEY Each stage race has a special leader's jersey so that the audience can see which cyclist is trying to defend his position at the top of the score board. The colour chosen for the leader's jersey is usually a colour that will remind the audience of the race's main sponsor. For example, the Giro d'Italia leader's jersey is pink because the magazine behind the race, *La Gazzetta dello Sport*, is printed on pink paper. In the Tour de France, the leader's jersey is yellow after the Tour's first organizer, the magazine *L'Auto*, which was sometimes printed on yellow paper. And in the Vuelta a España, the jersey is red. It's unclear why. The colour has changed from time to time over the years. First it was orange, then white, then back to orange, then white with red stripes, then yellow like in the Tour de France, then a yellow-gold colour. But since 2010, it's been red.

> ## "LIFE is like a ten-speed bicycle. Most of us have gears we never use."
>
> SNOOPY, *PEANUTS*

LYCRA is an often-ridiculed material that I barely thought about until I became the object of mockery myself after joining the group MAMIL – Middle-aged Men in Lycra. However, when I take stock of my rather modest collection of cycling clothes hanging in the garage, I can't find a single label that says "Lycra".

Research informs me that Lycra is the trademark of an artificial fibre with high elasticity. Like Spandex, the term is used across the world as a collective name for all kinds of glossy, durable synthetic clothes. Just as "Vespa" has come to mean any type of scooter.

Lycra was developed in 1958 by the chemical company DuPont, which is also behind brands such as Kevlar, Neoprene, Nylon and Teflon. The material behind Lycra is a polyester-polyurethane copolymer, if that means anything to you.

Lycra's journey into the cycling world is quite remarkable. First to wear a futuristic outfit of silver Lycra was East German Lothar Thoms when he won gold in the men's 1,000m at the Moscow Olympic Games in 1980. All his competitors still had relatively flattering silk jerseys and wool trousers. The following year everyone cycled in Lycra, but it had taken 22 years for the material to find its way into cycling. Even stranger perhaps is the fact that the pioneer of this American material was East German.

When I check what my favourite cycling jersey is made from, I see that it's polyester, nothing more nor less. So I decide to find out more.

At Craft Sportswear, a shipping container from China sits outside. Inside the building, Mattias Carlsson greets me. He's a retired racing cyclist and rode with both professional and national teams.

"But I haven't ridden in the Tour de France," he says before I even ask the question because he knows it's always coming.

"Who's the market for your cycling clothes?"

"It's a fragmented market, but we mostly produce form-fitting clothes for road cyclists. Sure, some MTB riders also buy our products, but not the most trendy items because they want looser-fitting garments. A ride up through a mountain forest to drink a beer; that's not us. A fast race, that's when you want to wear tight garments."

"Based on your own experience, how do today's cycling clothes differ from those of the past?"

"Quite a lot, actually. Today's clothes are better, properly fitted and more flexible. Previously, many garments had thick elasticated hems and cuffs. Now they're one piece and paper thin."

Yeah, that's probably right. Not that I have Mattias' experience – I'm older, but he's been cycling longer – but I've tried the retro jerseys. Firstly, because I think woollen jerseys are more beautiful, and secondly because, for the sake of the environment, I always try to choose materials not fabricated with hydrocarbons, which are often found in Lycra, polyester and other synthetic materials. But a rain shower or a heavy sweat in a wool sweater, and the wool immediately loses its shape and suddenly the tools in your back pocket are dangling down round your knees. It's also uncomfortable to wear.

"Another thing," says Mattias, "is that, today, jerseys aren't made of just a single material like they used to be. Now there are different fabrics in different places to achieve different functions. In one place, for ventilation, in another, wind protection, and so on. Each part may be manufactured in different ways."

"Is that why it's good to save clothing labels nowadays?"

"Yes, exactly. But if you like your jersey and want to find a similar one, it's not enough to look at the label that tells you what material it's made from. That tells you nothing about how the thread is spun, how the fabric is woven and so on."

Then Mattias explains that all Craft clothing is made in Asia, even though we are standing in an old weaver's workshop. Yes, all the clothes, except the club outfits. If a cycling club wants a new club jersey, these limited editions will be made in Romania.

"But everything is sketched and designed here. Once a new collection is finished, we will have a guy or a girl in size medium get on the bike we have upstairs to test the new garments. If the test results are to our satisfaction, we'll place an order in all different sizes and sometimes in three widths."

"Three widths?"

"Yes, though that's mainly for our pro jerseys. The pros are so incredibly skinny. If an amateur wants a similar jersey, there's a chance that his entire belly will hang out under the bottom. It's different in cycling because even if you have a big beer belly, you can still hang out with a bunch of other cyclists. That's not how it works in running."

"Do you also make different sizes tailored to the countries in which your clothes will be sold? People look a bit different around the world."

"No, all our patterns are based on typical European sizing. I understand what you mean, but our production is not so big and global that we need to adapt to different sizing around the world."

Back home, I go to the website of the company that made my favourite jersey - the labels have long been thrown away. It says that my contoured fit top has body framing technology and is made from Dry3d, Dry3pro microfiber and Dry3d titanium. So perhaps it's this Dry3 that makes my polyester jersey so good?

M

THE MADONNA DEL GHISALLO is the patron saint of cyclists. A church of the same name is located on a small mountain (also of the same name) not far from Lake Como in Italy.

Madonna del Ghisallo (the mountain) is on the route of the Tour of Lombardy cycle race and has also been featured several times in the Giro d'Italia. Ermelindo Vigano, the priest at the church of Madonna del Ghisallo, thought it would be appropriate to elevate Madonna del Ghisallo (the saint) as the cyclists' protector. Pope Pius XII also thought it was a good idea.

Madonna del Ghisallo (the church) houses a small bicycle museum where there's an eternal flame for all cyclists who have died. But mostly it burns for cyclist Fabio Casartelli from Como, Italy, who died in 1995 during a stage of the Tour de France. Casartelli's wrecked bicycle is also on display.

Similar churches consecrated to cycling include the Notre Dame des Cyclistes in Labastide-d'Armagnac, France, and the Santuario de Nuestra Señora de Dorleta in Salinas de Léniz in the Basque country.

MONEY It's possible to spend a lot of money on a racing bicycle. The question of how much to spend is, of course, a highly personal matter. The British newspaper the *Telegraph* conducted an interesting, albeit rather unscientific, test.

They borrowed four bikes in different price ranges, from £600 to £13,000. Then they asked a professional cyclist and a skilled amateur to test them around a one-mile track. The overall result for these two cyclists was that it cost an extra £400 to save one second around the track. That's an expensive second. Worth the price if it means winning the Tour, but less worthwhile if you're cycling only a few amateur team hours per week.

Even more interesting was the finding that the amateur's biggest time gain was achieved on the cheapest bike, the one that cost £600, followed by the second cheapest, at £1,200. After that, his time gains levelled out dramatically: even on the more expensive bikes he couldn't get much faster. The professional, on the other hand, barely registered any difference in time between the cheapest bikes. His biggest time gain occurred when he traded up from the bike costing £3,000 to the one with a price tag of £13,000. This is simply because a professional can dare to push a good bike through tight bends, and a professional has the ability to accelerate quickly, which is how these exclusive bikes are designed to be ridden.

Really expensive bikes don't help an amateur achieve better performance. It's wasted money. In other words, a zero second time gain for every extra £400.

THE MOUNTAIN It's just over there. I can see it in the distance, and it feels like the mountain can see me, too. It's extremely beautiful here in this part of Provence. In one direction, a flat landscape sloping down to the Mediterranean: vines, olive groves and fields of lavender. In the other direction, a mountain not to be taken lightly: Mont Ventoux. At first glance, it doesn't look so bad. Not sharp and steep, but soft and inviting. It's an impression that turns out to be both correct and misleading. The mountain is rather like a sumo wrestler: round and doughy in its contour but something you should avoid coming into contact with, if at all possible. Of course nobody really needs to cycle up a mountain. Nevertheless, I and countless others every year have travelled here to do exactly that.

I started in Malaucène, not the nearest route up the mountain, but I wanted to approach from the same direction as the cyclists in the Tour de France, via Bédoin. This is where all the graffiti starts; the names of famous cyclists are scribbled everywhere along the road. Further on, it trails off, leaving just the words "Go! Go!" in French. Eventually, just a single word: "Courage".

When I hired the bike, I inquired about the weather at the top. The man reluctantly typed something into his computer and said I'd have a sunny ride up.

"What about the wind?" I wondered, because Mont Ventoux actually means "the windy mountain".

"Ah, not too bad. Winds at 50kph (31mph)."

I had trouble figuring out exactly how fast that is; I understand it better in metres per second. But it sounded like a lot. To face a wall of wind gusting at 50km.

"How fast does the wind have to be to discourage cyclists?"

"Well, you can ride a bicycle in gusts of 100kph (62mph), *pas de problème*."

I should know better. It isn't a good idea to ask a guy hiring out bicycles about things that risk limiting his ability to make money. You'll never get an answer you can trust.

My ambition is modest, I think. I'm simply aiming to reach the top without stopping, how difficult can it be? It's only 22km (13.7 miles); pretty straightforward pedalling, right?

Quite soon I pass men on bikes standing by the side of the road. They look as if they're waiting for a slower teammate to catch up. They look down, send texts, make phone calls. But they're not fooling anyone. They've run out of energy and need a break. As I pass them, they hold their breath, hoping their out-of-breath wheezing doesn't give them away. It's mostly men. Most of the women I see are fulfilling a role of "support vehicle" for men. They drive past, stop, briefly take a picture of their brave man, scream "Go!" and "Courage!", jump back into their cars and drive on a little further to do the whole thing over again.

Before long, I too feel the temptation to stop. It's not a huge distance, but there aren't any flat stretches where you can catch your breath. It's 22,000 bloody metres uphill, *merde*! So, I keep at it. Winching myself up, little by little, obsessively checking the current incline on my GPS. After a while, an incline of seven percent seems okay, almost flat, and 11kph (7mph) feels fast.

Then I encounter a problem. The umbrella pine forest I've been riding through thins and I can see glimpses of open landscape, including the top of the mountain with its red tower sparkling in the sun. And that's when I realize that I have a thousand metres left, and I feel the energy just drain out of me. A thousand metres of elevation still to go. Soon after that, an indicator flashes on my GPS and warns me of the 17 percent slope ahead, which I can't even see the end of. Then the mountain beats me with its supremacy. The sumo wrestler has taken hold of me and it's no use struggling. My GPS thinks I've stopped because my speed sometimes drops to zero miles per hour. The psychological realization and physical barrier cause me to stop, get off the bike, hold onto a tree and try to get my breath back.

I sit on a rock for a while, drink water and think about this slope, how it's a measure of one's fitness. On a mountain, the incline really shows how fit you are. Clearly, I lack the fitness for 17 percent. That slope would be the end of me. I'm probably more of a 12 percent guy. That's why I'm having a rest.

Back in the saddle, the last few miles across the open, barren, moon-like landscape are demanding, but I keep on and I don't need to stop very often. Suddenly, I get my reward at the top with a heavenly view of Vaucluse and a proud selfie on social media.

Many people would consider riding back downhill to be a reward, too, but it's a bit too fast for my liking. I've seen professionals on television rush downhill at 90kph (56mph), but it's starting to get scary just over 50kph (31mph). So I lean on the brakes for large stretches until I reach the foot of the mountain and a café beside a babbling brook where they serve beer. I order a Grimbergen, though it seems ironic to drink a beer with a name that, in Swedish, sounds a bit like "grim mountain".

The second day, I cycle up the mountain in a single run. I'm almost alone cycling on this first Monday after the French holidays. I'm thinking about why I haven't had to stop and lean against a pine tree this time. First, I think it's because I'm riding a different route, up the north side this time, which is easier. The total ascent is the same, of course, but there are fewer brutal stretches and even a few flat stretches to recover your energy. But then I realize that it's the wind that is helping me up. I don't fully understand this until I'm almost at the top. Then I really feel the lift, thanks to the strong wind. But how strong is it really, I ask myself as I pass a cyclist coming the other way on his way down. He's riding extremely slowly, holding up four annoyed motorists behind him, and he gives me a pained smile.

On the mountain top the wind is literally blowing my bike away. I'm not kidding. I'm trying to stay in the saddle and the front wheel is rising up off the ground until suddenly I'm standing and the bike is practically vertical. I remember the bike hire guy and his "a hundred kilometres per hour is no problem" nonsense. Not to mention that it's cold, terribly cold, so I decide to make a start down the south side straight away.

As I begin to start off downhill, I realize I don't dare attempt it. The wind gusts have such power that I am afraid I'll be blown right over the stone balustrade and disappear down the side of the mountain. So, body hunched over, I decide to walk down while holding tightly on to my bike so it doesn't blow away like a kite. After a while, there are about 20 of us cyclists walking down Mont Ventoux, the windy mountain.

After a few miles I dare to ride again and cruise back toward Bédoin. Almost down in the small town, I pass two ambulances on their way up. Of course, they might not be going to help cyclists blown away on the mountain, but...

MOUNTAIN BIKE I bought a mountain bike (MTB) after watching the sport. Fun, I thought. Speeding along dirt roads; I can do that.

After buying an MTB online, I rode it for about 20 minutes on a trail, fell off four times, thought "what could possibly go wrong?" and signed up for a race the following weekend. When I crossed the finish line, both arms and legs were bleeding and I had a bruise the size of a large pizza. Strangely enough, I was happy with my efforts and almost pleased with the injuries which made me feel young. Don't ask me to explain, because I can't.

A year later, I'm riding in another MTB event and this time I'm not bleeding. I'm feeling good and I haven't even used the pain-relief cream that was distributed during registration. If I'm honest, I'm a cowardly mountain bike rider, and I mostly fall off when I come to a standstill; I lack the courage to really tackle the obstacles. I should have started 40 years ago...

This MTB event is part of a folk festival. We cycle in the woods, grill sausages and drink lemonade while incomprehensibly outdated music is booming from a loud speaker system and a slightly creepy announcer praises us and claps. Well, I suppose it's more fun than cycling or grilling sausages by yourself.

The creation of the mountain bike is usually attributed to a group of young people in California who modified regular men's bicycles for riding downhill in mountain terrain. This resulted in the birth of the bicycle manufacturer Specialized, who in 1981 launched the Stumpjumper. Looking at that bike now, it appears to be nothing more than a lightly modified man's bike, but the Stumpjumper's success was down to a stronger frame, wheels and tyres, 15 gears and a rugged design, not only because you could jump stumps, but because the bike was a good product that could be used most of the time – a real all-terrain bike.

Though it began as something of an all-purpose bicycle, the MTB has become increasingly specialized. The first Stumpjumper had no suspension at all; now you can get it with different levels of damping, both front and back. This applies to different sizes and widths of wheels. Since the sport of mountain biking has split into several different branches, specialization has continued to increase. Today, "mountain biking" is an umbrella term for a range of activities, including cross country, enduro, freeride, downhill, trial, dirt jumping, urban, street, single speed, mountain cross and north shore, as well as other variations I don't know of or whose purpose I don't understand.

The fact that mountain biking is believed to have originated in California has more to do with the fact that the Americans managed to coin a term for an old idea; cycling in rough terrain is actually a more venerable practice. The Rough Stuff Fellowship was started in Britain in the mid-1950s and almost the very next day there were Flemish people dragging their bikes over a muddy hill in the process of inventing what we now call cycle cross.

A MUSETTE is a small, lightweight fabric bag with a long shoulder strap, filled with drinks and energy bars and handed to road racers during a race. It's easier for a rider to grab than, for example, a water bottle and a pastry, and is temporarily worn over the shoulder. When the cyclist has placed the contents of the bag in his rear jersey pockets and bottle cage, the bag is dumped on the verge.

MUUR is Dutch for "wall", but is also a cycling term for a short, steep hill, often covered with cobblestones.

N

NUTRITION is the subject of endlessly recurring and slightly obsessive conversations between cyclists. That's why I arrange to meet Henrik Orre, who has the fairly unusual job title of "cycling chef". Today, he works primarily for the British pro team Team Sky, but he's also author of the book *Vélochef – Food for Training and Competition*.

I start by reading Eddy Merckx's typical menu: "Breakfast: cheese, ham, toast, venison with juniper berries. During a race: tea, juice, apples, dried fruit, sandwiches with onion marmalade and raisins. For dinner: soup, fish, pasta, more venison and green beans – always green beans. How would that go down today?"

"Okay," says Henrik, "It would be okay. But maybe not with venison. The riders would probably think it was too heavy, a little hard to digest. They would rather have lighter food that feels easy on the stomach. Today, most riders get their protein from eggs."

"What else, besides eggs?"

"A little porridge, smoothies, a small amount of bread, a salad and then eggs, like scrambled eggs or an omelette. If it's a really tough stage of a race, I offer them a rice dish. But no pasta. In a three-week race, we may have pasta only once for dinner because the riders prefer that."

"No pasta?"

"No, the guys are so careful about their weight. They know what an extra pound of weight costs them in a mountain stage. They know their ideal weight and keep an eye on it. But of course, that depends on which team you're working with. I've seen Italian teams pushing pasta for breakfast. Likewise, I serve almost no milk products to avoid the fat, and no refined sugar. If they need something sweet, I use honey or agave."

Henrik Orre comes from a Norwegian cycling family and also cycles himself, although he never reached the level his brother and father achieved.

"My father, Magne, came fourth in the team time trials at the 1972 Olympic Games. He still talks about that race. The team was hit by two flat tyres. Otherwise they would have reached the podium."

Instead of riding professionally, Henrik quickly built himself an impressive career.

"I worked a long time as a chef, but I wanted to do something else. It became too stressful, and we wanted to start a family. So I began looking at what else was out there."

It turns out that the Orre family still had contact with the Norwegian cycling team.

"Two Norwegians were riding for Team Sky, so they recommended me as chef. And that's how I got to this point. Next year, I'll be working with Team Sky for 120 days."

We talk a little about the professionals and their cycling physique with minimal subcutaneous fat.

"They want a light upper body, no muscle in the wrong place. Many Norwegian cyclists are told to stop cross-country skiing in the winter. Cyclists don't need those muscles. Unless you're a sprinter, you only need muscles as a kind of protection."

"Protection?"

"Yes, a guy like Alexander Kristoff wants a body that can handle crashing at 50kph (31mph) and then starting again the next day."

"Jesus."

Then we talk about nutritional intake during a race. I mention that I saw on Henrik's twitter account that Chris Froome had liked his homemade rice cakes.

"Well, even if I don't decide exactly what the riders are going to eat during a race, I stock the support vehicle with different things. Rice cakes in small packages are really appreciated. Banana and Nutella is always an easy one."

Sometimes Henrik's job is to make sure the guys actually eat. Henrik says it's important to vary their diet, and to make it look appetizing and fresh. Exhausted athletes can easily skip a meal because they're too tired to feel hungry.

"It's clear that they also eat bars and stuff themselves full of energy gels. But that's because it's easier to keep an eye on your intake if you use an energy drink than it is if you're eating the marmalade that Merckx ate. It's extremely important that the riders eat as much as they do in a race. One year, Froome missed a climb up Alpe d'Huez because of low blood sugar. There was a problem with the support vehicle. He lost thirty seconds. But he was four minutes in front so it didn't impact him that much anyway."

"When you ride yourself, how do you approach your own nutrition?"

"Nothing that unusual. A little diluted juice and some rice cakes are definitely enough. When I rode, they'd try to give me some energy packs. "You need a gel every half an hour, and a bar," they said. "No way," I said. "Good god, all this hysteria about supplements – grab a banana and drink some water!"

Then Henrik describes the logistics required to feed a cycling team for several weeks when they are sleeping in a different place every night. He explains that the food he cooks is just for the cyclists (everyone else has to settle for hotel food) and tells me about the kitchen and the big freezers in the bus and the importance of knowing where the food comes from.

"For example, all meat should be traceable. We only buy organic meat from a single farm in England. You shouldn't have to worry about ingesting banned substances in your food."

As well as feeding the Norwegian national cycling team and Team Sky, Henrik has worked as a TV chef in Norway. On one assignment he followed the route of the Tour de France and cooked local recipes based on the different stages of the race. In addition, he's the brains behind the menu at the trendiest cycle café in London, Rapha.

"It was a one-off job. But there may be more that comes with it. The menu might also be used in other cafés that they are about to open. I managed to get products from Fabrique, the Swedish stone oven bakery, on the menu. That was pretty cool."

ONE HUNDRED AND TWO The age at which Frenchman Robert Marchand climbs off his bike after breaking his own record, set two years before, in the 100 year-old-plus age group. The new record: 26,927 metres (16¾ miles) in an hour.

Monsieur Marchand started racing at 14 years old but under a false name because he was too young. "My advice to all," he says to the press in the velodrome of Saint-Quentin-en-Yvelines, "young and old, is to keep moving. I exercise every day. Some people start playing cards when they reach 80, which makes them stiff. Not me. I've never been able to sit still..."

OTB is short for "over the bars" or "over the handlebars." It's used when talking about those who involuntarily leave the bike that way.

OUDENAARDE After leaving Italy, I arrive by train in Oudenaarde, Flanders. From the train window, I realize that everything is different. I see cycle paths along canals and fields. I see road signs just for cyclists. I see whole families out on Sunday bike rides.

In Italy, it was just traffic chaos. While driving a car, you are either waiting in a traffic jam on the autostrada, waiting in a traffic jam on a main road or waiting in a traffic jam in a suburb of a city centre that is no longer accessible by car. Cycling in Italy is generally regarded as being hazardous to your life: intense traffic and an almost complete lack of cycle lanes. It's not the sort of place to go on a bike ride with your family.

Stijn Van Houdt from Visit Flanders is waiting for me in the hotel lobby, with an extra bike in hand. We ride out of Oudenaarde along the river Schelde, packed so tightly with barges that you might think it was a canal. It's flat along the river, obviously, but the terrain is flat in every direction, as far as I can see. It's hard to believe that any challenges await. Stijn pedals calmly while telling me about De Ronde van Vlaanderen, the Tour of Flanders, which now finishes in Oudenaarde.

"The first race was held in 1913. As in Italy and France, it was a sports paper that started it, wanting more advertising and more readers. *Sportwereld* was the paper and the driving force behind it was Karel Van Wijnendaele, one of the shareholders."

We pass some other cyclists, see a barge carrying 18 containers and some cows. Then we come to the first climb, Paterberg, and Stijn gives me some instructions.

"Stay in the saddle, relax your arms and hands, hold the handlebars as if you had a newborn chick in your hands. Try to find a good route; there is a big difference between *cobblestones* and cobblestones. Do not be ashamed to sit down. Better cyclists than you have had to do that."

No way, I think. Something I never do is give up. Which, of course, is an idiotic attitude and the reason I don't get involved with sports more dangerous than cycling.

Stijn sets the pace. I keep up behind him. It's fine until we start cycling on the cobblestones where I immediately encounter a problem. I fail to find a good line, lose speed, stand up (despite Stijn's instructions) and my rear wheel immediately starts spinning on the wet rocks. I sit down, a long way back in the saddle, making my front wheel lighten. I'm starting to get frustrated about my failure to cope with the conditions. The incline is at least 20 percent, but the hill is not very long; the climb right to the top of Paterberg is no longer than 360m (394 yards). Still, I'm completely exhausted when I get up there and stop next to Stijn, who looks pretty much unbothered.

"The Tour now has 17 uphills like this. Some, like Paterberg, are ridden twice."

After Paterberg we have a stretch of pleasant cycling before it's time for the next climb and the next and the next after that. It's like a kind of interval training where I soon learn that it isn't the incline that's the worst part, but rather the length of the stretch. For example, Oude Kwaremont is a real monster even though the average incline is only 3.5 percent. The length of the climb is 2,600m (2,843 yards) and the conditions on the cobblestone section are purely medieval. Some of the cobblestones are fairly flat stone blocks which are easy to cycle over, while others are what the Flemish people call *kinderkopjes* ("children's skulls"), large round rocks where each one feels like an obstacle in itself.

We cycle into Ronse for a coffee but it's just gone 11:00 in the morning when, according to Flemish practice, you don't have to drink coffee but can have a beer instead. Stijn has to order in French because we've now ridden over a linguistic border and found ourselves in the French-speaking part of Belgium.

"What do you think?" Stijn wonders. "The Tour is known as *Vlaanderens mooiste* – Flanders' finest. Do you agree?"

I just nod feebly and take a big, well-deserved gulp of beer. On one hand, it's insanity to ride on cobblestones, but on the other hand, it's no stranger than other types of cycling that challenge boundaries. How far can I ride? How high can I ride? Those questions are more common but may not be all that different from the one here in Flanders: What's the most wretched ground surface I can cycle on? No wonder that cycle cross is a big sport here.

"The Tour of Flanders has always been a race about nationalism," Stijn says, as if the French-speaking waitress had reminded him of it. "It was about showing that Flanders could also produce talented, brave and determined athletes. That this country at land's end was not populated with just poor, low-skilled farmers."

We drink our beer and watch other cyclists arrive in or leave the main square.

Stijn tells me some anecdotes about the Tour of Flanders. The fact that the race continued to be held even during German occupation, which caused suspicions of collaboration. A story about the strong wind which once blew away the banner that marked the finish line and knocked the Italian leader Nino Defilippis off his pace, helping British cyclist Tom Simpson to sneak by and steal his victory. And another tale from 1969, when a frustrated Eddy Merckx rode like a madman and finally won the race he had so far failed to win, eventually crossing the finishing line five and a half minutes before the rider in second place.

"The Tour takes place in early April," he continues, "and has become known for its bad weather; for rain and mud, wind and cold. But this is not true if you look at the statistics. Two-thirds of the races so far have actually had fine weather. But the audience would prefer to see some rough conditions."

"How big is cycling as a sport here?"

"Very big, maybe the biggest, in line with football. There are usually around seven hundred thousand people lining the roads to catch a glimpse of the Tour – more than one in ten of the population. The rest are at home watching it on television."

We leave Ronse and cruise up some small climbs, passing through lovely villages with newly renovated houses where the architects haven't been afraid to mix new and old styles. It's an extremely beautiful landscape for cycling.

Stijn stops and points to a sign that says "Koppenberg" and then down at a mark on the road.

"You can register for a time chip at the Centrum Ronde van Vlaanderen, the Tour of Flanders centre, to measure your time up Koppenberg. Then you can compare it to others online. Koppenberg is the worst, just so you know. No other incline has seen so many professionals forced off their bikes. The worst was in 1987 when Jesper Skibby, a Danish cyclist, wobbled up the hill and got his front wheel run over by a race steward's car, then the other riders followed him down. It was a mess. Everyone was off their bikes. Then it's impossible to start again. 'This hill is ridiculous,' someone said, 'We want to ride with ladders on the backs of our bikes.' Okay, up we go!"

Stijn starts slowly and methodically grinding up Koppenberg. The road has trees down the sides. Leaves have fallen. There's still dew from last night. No matter what I do, my rear wheel slips and my front wheel is raised up and the children's skulls seem to rise up from the ground with the intention of stopping my progress. And that's on the steepest section, with a 22 percent incline, which would be tough on any surface but it's terrible here. In the end, however, I make it to the top.

"Here," says Stijn, pointing to a flat part, "usually the race is decided here. The person who still has some strength left after Koppenberg wins."

Then Stijn takes off again. After a few minutes we come to another section of cobblestones.

"You have to increase your speed, a bit over thirty, so that it becomes bearable. Then it feels more like you are hovering above the cobbles," Stijn said, somewhat comfortingly.

I never reach that hovering stage as I try to keep up with Stijn. I'm thinking about everything that can come loose: teeth fillings, knee caps, hips. Right about now "Flanders' finest" sounds like a really bad nickname. But after a few hundred metres, it'll be tarmac again. I'll quickly forget the mischievous cobblestones because everything else here is fine. Flanders' finest.

P

PANNIER *Panier* was initially just a French word for "basket". Nowadays, pannier (with an added "n"), is a fairly international term for a bicycle bag.

Bike bags come in many sizes, styles and materials. The most practical and weather resistant are made of woven plastic, while the most beautiful, but often heavy and impractical, are made of leather. In between are those made of waxed canvas or cotton.

You can get bags that hang on the front or rear rack of a bike, handlebar bags that hang loose or rest on the front rack, and bags that fasten to the saddle, seat post or bike frame. Disposable cardboard panniers are available in some countries. These are designed for the impulsive cyclist who, instead of packing things into a grocery bag, would rather make a cardboard pannier as and when it is needed, to be hung over the front or rear rack.

Those who go on cycling holidays usually make sure that their panniers hang low, as this gives better stability than a higher bag, which will make the bike wobble.

PARIS–ROUBAIX is one of the more legendary races. It's also called the "Hell of the North." The reason for this is that one-fifth of the 250km (155 mile) course is run on cobblestones. On top of the merciless terrain, the race is usually held on the first Sunday of April, when it is often cold and rainy.

I pick up my rental bike at Lille station and set a course for Roubaix. The race doesn't pass through Lille, so I have to ride east to join the route. I've made it easy for myself by choosing to ride only the final stretch of the race, about 15km (9.3 miles). My city bike is heavy and sluggish, but it has wide, softly inflated tyres which are forgiving of the rocky terrain. Nevertheless, at the road sign proclaiming "Roubaix 9km", I, like most competitors in the race, size up the road to see if it's possible to bypass the cobblestones. This is because it has quickly started to feel like both the bike and myself are going to shake loose all of our joints and collapse in a pile of spare parts. All of the photos of the Paris–Roubaix show cyclists looking as if they've rolled in mud like water buffalo, because they have tried to escape the cobblestones by riding through ditches.

For all of these reasons, the word "Roubaix" is often used in product names to emphasize that, for example, a frame is resistant to impact or has particularly durable wheels, sometimes both. A friend of mine allegedly had wheels specially built for the Paris–Roubaix by one of the Fåglum brothers, who won an Olympic silver medal. The rims of the wheels were made from laminated wood, which has resilient properties that make it easier to ride over cobblestones.

Cobblestones are often referred to by their French name, *pavés*, meaning "paved." This type of paving goes back to the days before the invention of concrete and tarmac, and is made exclusively of individual stones. Pavé is another word frequently found in product names for bicycle frames, lights and tyres, as well as a very trendy cycling café in Barcelona.

The last of the 28 sections of cobblestones in the race is only 300m (328 yards) long but probably feels like three hundred miles by the time you've ridden the rest of the course.

PARTS The number of parts that end up on the garage floor if you take apart a gearless bicycle: 105.

Of course, there are bicycles with more or fewer parts, but 105 is a fair average if you count certain features as a single part, such as the chain, the headset and the spokes on the front wheel.

If, on the other hand, you count every constituent part that makes up a bicycle as a single piece, the number is about 755.

A PIG is a concrete barrier intended to prevent cyclists from colliding with motorists, but more often than not, it results in cyclists colliding with the pig instead.

PIRACY also occurs in the bicycle world. Expensive carbon fibre frames, in particular, are copied and sold through different channels.

You can find discussion threads online that explore whether the pirated frames are as good as the original, if they're identical and if they are priced properly. I disagree with such discussions. We know that Asia, in particular, is a leader in piracy, as well as being environmentally questionable and degrading in its treatment of its labour force. If you purchase a branded product, you are guaranteed a certain amount of transparency. The brand manufacturers have journalists, trade unions and other organizations monitoring them, organizations such as the UN, Worldwatch Institute and Save the Children. Do you really want to buy a product from a company that circumvents all environmental laws, uses child labour and vulnerable adults working in slave-like conditions? If so, buy a pirated product. If that's not what you want to support, then you should give your business to a branded company that abides by regulations.

It doesn't just have to be about carbon fibre frames, either. All products that are suspiciously cheap might be attractive to customers, but usually they can only maintain these low prices because they're manufactured under unacceptable conditions. That must-have bicycle jersey with your favourite team logo that cost almost nothing to buy was probably manufactured in a mafia-controlled factory room in a basement outside of Naples by an illegal immigrant who works long hours for very little pay.

PROCESSIONARY MOTHS caused the strangest bicycle accident I've ever known, in the spring of 2015. In their larval stage, the caterpillars of these moths march in large numbers, single file, looking for leaves to eat. Around 20 of these caterpillars, marching in single file, can stretch across the entire width of a road. In some cases, there may be tens of thousands of these caterpillars simultaneously crossing the tarmac.

That was what happened just outside Seville, as a bike race was passing through. Three hundred cyclists thundered through a huge accumulation of processionary moths and their fine, irritant hairs caused severe skin irritation and breathing difficulties. Over two hundred cyclists were hospitalized.

A PSYCH-LIST is a person who cycles without regard to other traffic.

A QUADRACYCLE is a four-wheeled bike. Originating in 1853, the quadracycle was partly a solution to the balancing problems that the two-wheelers were plagued with, and partly a more social means of transport, as it usually had more than one seat.

Over the years, some bicycle cars have been built with four wheels, but they more often have three wheels.

Today, the quadracycle is usually found in amusement parks and on seafronts, offering a novel experience to tourists.

THE QUEEN STAGE refers to the fiercest, toughest and most unsettling stage of a race, or the highlight of the course. Generally, it's often the most demanding and highest mountain. In Italian: *Il tappone*.

QUICKSILVER The American feature film from 1986 with Kevin Bacon in the lead role. A little like *Dirty Dancing*, but on two wheels. (*See* "Fixie" for more about the movie.)

R

RAIN You can ride a bike in the rain, but you need to consider a few points:

- ➤ It can be most slippery just after it has started raining. Liquids that have dripped on the road from motor vehicles are wetted by the rain and add to the slipperiness.
- ➤ If you have traditional rim brakes, they do not work as well in the rain as disc brakes.
- ➤ Parts of the road surface you would usually choose to ride on – like smooth, fine concrete – can now be the most slippery parts.
- ➤ Avoid manhole covers and anything else made of metal.
- ➤ Splashing is unavoidable. Give yourself plenty of room in really bad weather.
- ➤ Wear weatherproof clothing. It's said that some fabrics protect against rain while staying breathable, so that even when you are sweating, you stay dry. Maybe that's true, but I've never found anything that works reliably. If you aren't on a bike, a plastic coat and rubber boots work well.
- ➤ Keep calm, and even calmer round the bends.
- ➤ Wear extra reflectors or a neon jacket. Motorists have windscreen wipers, but their visibility still deteriorates in rain.
- ➤ Ride quickly through large puddles. It's always fun.

RANDONNEUR "I'd like a bike like that," I thought the first time I encountered a randonneur. Of course, I'd said that many times before and have many times again since, but that particular randonneur was different. I thought, "That bike is me."

The bike I saw in the picture looked like something between a road racing bike and a tourer, with light steel frame, narrow mudguards and a small front rack to hold a bag. On a randonneur, you could head out any time, be away for a while and come back when you feel like it.

It's a beautiful word, randonneur. It's French, of course, and means "rambler" or "tourer", with the emphasis being on making a journey for pleasure. This isn't a commuting bike or a racing bike, this is a bike for leisure.

As I begin to embrace the concept of the randonneur, I realize that what I first thought of as a freedom machine for lone wolves appears to be mostly used by long-distance cyclists for club activities.

A randonnée turns out to be a long bike ride of around 200km (124 miles). Organized, yes, but the idea is that the cyclist should look after himself from start to finish, without security or support vehicles. A randonnée is also called a *brevet* ("ticket") because of the stamp card the cyclist brings with him to prove that he has passed certain controls or checkpoints along the route.

There also appears to be something called "audax". It is a variation on the randonnée where you cycle in a group with breaks for meals. The finest is the Paris–Brest–Paris race, which is 1,200km (746 miles) long. It started in 1891 and takes place every four years. Or perhaps the best is La 1001 Miglia, starting and finishing in the Milanese suburb of Nerviano and covering 1,623km (1,008 miles) of beautiful Italian countryside in between. Or maybe it's the Boston–Montreal–Boston. Well, it's not easy to say which is best. But to make things confusing, the term "audax" in Britain refers to a solo cycling race.

When I search the web for bicycles used in these long events, they're called a lot of different things, but I rarely see the kind of randonneur I first fell for. I can only find the usual carbon fibre frames with titanium screws and aerodynamic spokes and back pockets full of horrible-tasting energy gels. Which, of course, doesn't stop me from wanting to buy a randonneur.

But then, after seeing a British documentary about The Highlands, Glens and Western Isles audax (1,205km/749 miles, 18,000m/5,905ft of ascent, 100 hours to complete the course), I completely change my mind about these events. Despite everything, a randonnée through an extremely beautiful landscape actually seems like a very attractive option, even if the scale of the gruelling event is a little crazy. But that's as it should be, I suppose.

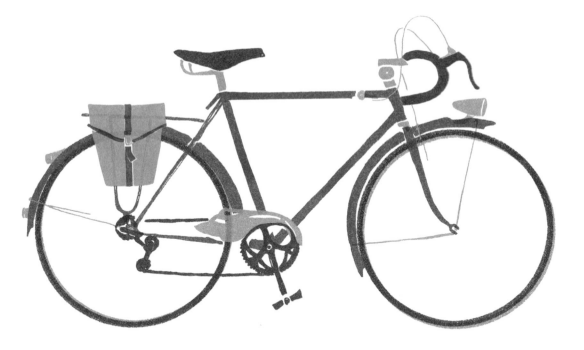

A RECUMBENT BICYCLE stands in a storehouse. Olof is selling it, because he bought the wrong one. Not the wrong model, but the incorrect seat height. Olof's new recumbent bike stands next to the old one. It looks exactly the same and is the same make, just slightly lower.

"I started by testing my father-in-law's. He has two. The model suited me. I work as a gardener and I commute all year round. I tried all sorts of bicycles. Even a fixie."

Recumbent bicycles have been around since the 19th century. Throughout cycling history, there have always been those who think that regular bikes are the wrong shape, that sitting upright and pedalling leads to greater air resistance and poorer power transmission. All the speed records, these people claim, are set with recumbent bicycles. There are recumbent bicycles where you lie on your front and look like you're crawling along, and then there are others where you lie back in a similar position as you would be on a rowing machine.

The role of recumbent cyclists as outsiders – "We cycle better than you do" – was reinforced in 1934 when they were forbidden to compete against regular cyclists, and they're not even allowed to participate in non-competitive events.

Olof's bicycle is certainly unusual but not unique: a reclining seat in carbon fibre, aluminium frame and a bottom bracket that sits higher than the rider's backside.

"Why a recumbent bike?" I wonder.

"I needed a comfortable bike that I could carry bags on. Because I don't have a car, I have to be able to do the shopping and pick up the children from school on my way home from work."

I can understand what he means about comfort, but when Olof talks about the bike's ability to carry bags, initially I don't understand what he means. It's only when he begins to hang bags on the bicycle that everything becomes clear. With the bottom bracket so high up, there's a long frame to make use of. Olof can fit six big bags plus a child seat on the bike. Now I understand what he means about baggage capacity.

"It actually works even better with proper packing. A lower centre of gravity."

"Cool," I say, impressed. "But in terms of cycling, isn't a recumbent bicycle more difficult?"

"Not really. You have a slightly restricted view, and when you have to stop at a red light, it's further down to the ground from the pedals. But you get used to it."

After a brief pause, Olof asks a question.

"But what do you think when you see a recumbent cyclist in town?"

"To be honest, I think it looks a little strange. But that's because there are so few of you. It's hard to get used to it."

"Exactly. People think we're just clowning around. That part I never seem to get used to. For example, I stop next to a taxi to point out that it's parked in the cycle lane and the taxi driver says, "Yeah, you're the one riding that crazy thing. What is that anyway?" You're reduced to a daft man on a daft bike with daft opinions. A Muppet on his Muppet cycle. A person whose opinions don't count."

ROULEUR is French for a cyclist who performs best on flat or moderately hilly terrain. A rouleur comes into his own in competitions like the Paris–Roubaix and the Tour of Flanders.

S

TO SALMON is a cycling term that means to cycle down a one-way street in the wrong direction, against the current. Which, of course, is illegal. Which, of course, should not be illegal.

SCALATORE is Italian for cyclists who are good at riding up steep slopes. From the word *scala*, meaning "stairs". The French use the word *grimpeur*, meaning "climber".

SCANDIUM is a rare earth element and metal which can be combined with aluminium to make an alloy which is 50 percent stronger and more durable than pure aluminium.

This element (SC, number 21 in the periodic table) was discovered in 1879 by Lars Fredrik Nilson, a chemistry professor in Uppsala. The place where he first found scandium was in a mine at Resarö near Stockholm. Seven of the world's elements have been discovered in this mine. All of them have been given names related to their place of discovery. Scandium is, of course, named in honour of Scandinavia.

"SE SI FRENA, NON SI VINCE."
(If you brake, you don't win.)
MARIO CIPOLLINI, CYCLIST

SELF-HEALING TYRE SEALANT is now available and promises a puncture-free existence. This puncture fluid, which quickly reseals a newly opened hole, works in both inner tubes and tubular tyres. The disadvantage is that the liquid makes the tyre a little heavier and it doesn't work as well on highly inflated racing tyres as it tends to leak out of the hole before it can block it. It works best on less inflated mountain bike tyres, where it can help the cyclist get home without having to fix a puncture in the woods.

SHAVED LEGS are common among professional cyclists. The view that no major competition in modern times has been won with unshaved legs is considered to be gospel truth. But at the same time, few people actually believe that shaving really makes a cyclist faster. Those who still shave their legs cite Chester Kyle's scientifically dubious study, which appeared in a 1987 issue of *Bicycling* magazine. Kyle claimed that shaved legs reduced drag by 0.6 percent, resulting in a few seconds advantage in a 40km (25 mile) high-speed race.

Therefore, the majority of people who've shaved over the years have done it because they didn't dare risk losing a few seconds. Other reasons include: it's easier to get a massage if your legs aren't hairy; it's easier to clean a wound; it's easier to remove bandages and tape; it feels nice in freshly laundered sheets; and one's partner thinks it looks sexy.

But recently Mark Cote and Chris Yu, who call themselves "aerodynamic gurus" at Specialized, succeeded in finding a handful of unshaven riders, got them in a wind tunnel, and asked them to cycle for a while. They then repeated the test with shaved legs. According to these gurus, time gains were measured between 50 and 80 seconds over a distance of 40km (25 miles).

A single test is not enough to say the results are scientifically conclusive. But until a scientist takes up the baton and succeeds in reproducing the results of Specialized's test, no professional will even consider the idea of cycling with unshaven legs. And Rapha will continue to sell special shaving cream for cyclists.

SLOW PUNCTURE The youth of today doesn't even know what this is! So you can no longer use the term as a metaphor for a person who gradually loses power and energy.

For a long time, I grumbled about the fact that my daughters couldn't fix a punctured tyre until I realized it was obsolete knowledge. It wasn't really worth learning. I no longer remember the last time we had a flat tyre in my family, and we have about ten bicycles in use.

Better tyres and wheel rims have eliminated the need for a job I learned to do before I started school:

1. Remove the tyre from the wheel with, ideally, a tyre lever, or in worst case scenario, a screwdriver.

2. Pump a little air into the tube; immerse it in a bucket of water to see where the air bubbles are coming from, thereby finding the hole.

3. Dry the tyre and try to remember where the hole was, then mark it with a ballpoint pen.

4. Apply a special puncture-repair glue to the tube. Once dry, stick the patch on the tube.

5. Fit the tube back inside the tyre and push the bead of the tyre back into the rim.

6. Pump the tyre up fully again; ride around a bit and discover that air is still slowly leaking out.

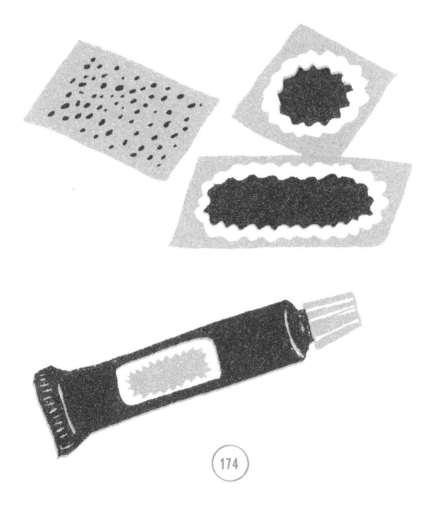

7. Shout "Flat tyres! I hate flat tyres!" And then repeat the whole sequence from Step 1. Young people today rarely have to go through this process. The last time I went looking for puncture-repair glue, I found no one sold it any more. It had been replaced by self-adhesive patches.

SLOW ROLL began in Detroit. Having a leisurely group ride was one of the ways to bring people together in this bankrupt city. But it was also a way to show that the bicycle could be an alternative to the car and that rebuilding Detroit doesn't necessarily have to be based on four-wheeled vehicles.

The phenomenon of Slow Roll has spread throughout the world. People ride for a bit, have fun and hang out. Usually, a Slow Roll ends with a group coffee. To me, the Slow Roll movement is a subtle protest against giving priority to car drivers.

SONGS ABOUT BICYCLES

1. "BICYCLE RACE", QUEEN, 1978. Freddie Mercury said he was inspired by the Tour de France. Others claimed that the word "bicycle" was a euphemism for "bisexual," as bisexuality was something Freddie Mercury was very open about.

   The music video for "Bicycle Race" shows 50 naked girls cycling around Wimbledon Stadium. The video was censored due to the nudity, and the bicycle company that loaned the bikes refused to take them back.

2. "NINE MILLION BICYCLES", KATIE MELUA, 2005. Two minutes into the music video, there's a still image of the Forbidden City in Beijing. Katie Melua doesn't come any closer to the Chinese capital than that.

3. "BROKEN BICYCLES", TOM WAITS, 1982. The song is part of the soundtrack to Francis Ford Coppola's movie *One from the Heart*. The film was a kind of music video, fully recorded in the studio, and expanded to a feature film. The film had high cult status because of the trio of Coppola, Waits and Nastassja Kinski, but it wasn't very good. It cost twenty-five million dollars to make and earned barely seven hundred thousand. I don't remember a single bicycle.

4. "TOUR DE FRANCE", KRAFTWERK, 1983. Released as a single, the song has since been recorded and remixed at least 15 times. It's said that the members of Kraftwerk are themselves

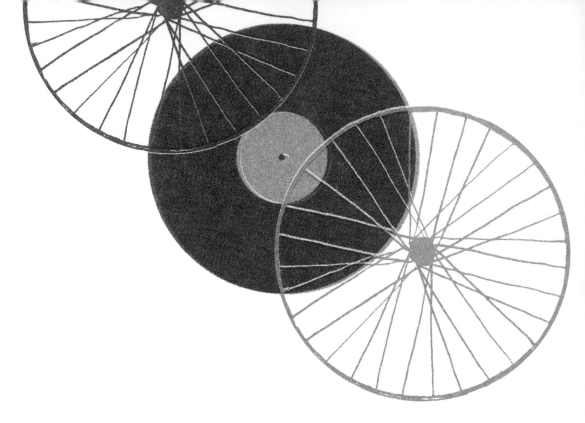

enthusiastic cyclists. They posed as cyclists on the record cover, and when on tour, they apparently ask to be dropped a few miles from their destination so that they can cycle the last bit. But with Kraftwerk you never know what's truth and what's myth. The same goes for the alleged similarity between Kraftwerk's music and cycling; the same symbiosis between body and tool, *Die Mensch-maschine.* At any rate, it's an extremely stylish cover.

5. "LES BICYCLETTES DE BELSIZE", ENGELBERT HUMPERDINCK, 1968. "Les Bicyclettes de Belsize" is, despite the name, a British theme song to a short film of the same name. The film is about 30 minutes long, almost completely without dialogue. The main character is a young man who crashes into a billboard and falls in love with the woman in the picture. His bike is a yellow mini-bike, a Raleigh RSW 16.

Belsize Park is an area of London, but none of the movie is filmed there. Why the title is in French is also unknown, especially with singer Humperdinck's peculiar French pronunciation. Mireille Mathieu sang a French version of the song.

6. "LA BICYCLETTE", YVES MONTAND, 1968. The song is about freedom, summer, grit roads, flowers, grasshoppers, frogs, and

being hand-in-hand with Paulette, who is eight years old – if you're brave enough to ride a bike, you're brave enough for anything.

7. "BELLEZZE IN BICICLETTA", AMEDEO ESCOBAR, 1951. Translated as "Chicks on Bicycles" by my local Swedish distributers but generally known as "Beauties on Bicycles", this is both a song and a film. The film was light, Italian comedic fare; two beautiful women from Milan are on their way to Totò's famous theatre in Rome. But the bus breaks down and they're forced to ride a bike – God, what a daft premise.

The title song surpassed the mediocre film and did well. "Bellezze in Bicicletta" seems to be featured on every collection of classic Italian pop songs – over thirty versions are available on iTunes.

8. "EL ANGEL DE A BICICLETA", MERCEDES SOSA, 2009. Argentinean Mercedes Sosa was a well-known political folk singer. For her views, she was banned, imprisoned and forced into exile in Spain.

"El Angel de la Bicicleta" is about a riot which took place during the Argentinian economic crisis in 2001 when 35-year-old Pocho Lepratti was shot dead by the police. Pocho Lepratti worked as a volunteer helping disadvantaged children. After the murder, the musician León Gieco wrote the song El Angel de la Bicicleta ("the angel on the bicycle") as a tribute to Pocho, who always travelled around the poor neighbourhoods on two wheels.

You can still find graffiti depicting an angel on a bike, along with Pocho's last words, which also became the song's chorus:

Bajen las armas
que aquí solo hay pibes comiendo!

Which can be translated as: "Lower your weapons, there are only children eating here!"

SRAM is one of the world's largest and greatest bicycle components manufacturers and is located in Chicago. I've just driven here from New York along the Lincoln Highway – but that's another story.

Michael Zellman leads me out on the roof terrace.

"Nice view, right?"

I look out over the city, the windy city, the city of meatpackers, skyscrapers and the Sears Tower, which, at 527m (1,729ft), was the highest in the world for 25 years after its construction in 1973. Nowadays it's called the Willis Tower. Strange. Like renaming the Eiffel Tower.

"But we're moving soon," says Michael, pointing to another large brick building that probably also once served as a factory or a warehouse. "The same building that Google is in. People tell me it's cool, but I don't know."

Then Michael shows me around. If there's one thing that is cool, it's SRAM's premises, that creative mess that happens when you mix employees who have computers at their workstations with those who have screwdrivers, drills and wrenches on theirs, all in an open-plan office. In addition, there are bikes everywhere and the aroma of espresso wafting through the air.

"See, we have our own little test track," says Michael, pointing to a painted cycle path that goes for about 50m (55 yards), before making a tight turn around an elevator shaft. "It is not the big, serious tests we do here, but the people who are developing new products often want to test what they've just screwed together. They're impatient. Some of these laps can be really good."

We move on. No one has an office door, except the boss. We pass a room with a big television screen.

"We watch the Tour de France in here in the mornings."

"How many teams are using your gear in the race this year?"

"Just three. But good teams," Michael emphasizes.

The reason for this is probably that SRAM didn't really get onboard when electronics were becoming popular. A few years ago, they had nine teams on the tour.

"But now we're catching up," says Michael, "we just didn't want to put anything out before we were confident it was really good. And SRAM's eTap is really good."

Maybe so. But a few days after my visit, Vincenzo Nibali rolled out onto the Champs Elysées on a bicycle with Campagnolo gears. The year before, Nibali's team Astana had run on SRAM. But if Astana switched to Campagnolo for the sake of electronics, it's a bit ironic because Nibali was one of the few cyclists who kept the older mechanical system.

Michael continues rattling off facts as we move on. They have 2,700 employees, growth is fuelled primarily by buying other brands: Sachs, Rock Shox, Avid, Truvativ, Zipp. But it's clear that the company is still about innovation.

"We have over two hundred patents," says Michael, when we sit down for a chat, "but everything started with the Grip Shift."

The Grip Shift (or twist shift) is operated by rotating the hand grip on the handlebars, and was developed in 1987 by three guys behind SRAM. They believed so strongly in their invention, that they started their own business instead of trying to sell the idea to any of the giants in the industry.

"That was, of course, insane. But it worked. As early as 1994, SRAM had sold more than ten million twist shifts."

It should be mentioned that in 1992 Shimano, with a seemingly identical product, made its own version of the twist shift that could be operated with the hands still on the handlebars. Since then, the two companies have repeatedly clashed in patent infringement suits.

"Actually," says Michael, pointing to a photo on a wall, "the first twist shifts were on racing bikes. People don't remember them today. But after that, it became more and more a gadget for mountain bikes."

It's also on the mountain bike side that SRAM has performed best. Now they have around 50 percent of that market while they only have 20 percent on the racing side.

We take the elevator down so that Michael can show me the twist shift. In a tunnel-like corridor we pass an open door. Inside, a man tinkers with a piece of aluminium. I stop and ask him some questions. A little reluctantly at first, he describes different types of aluminium with different kinds of properties. As our conversation progresses he becomes more and more enthusiastic about his own work and then he switches to the topic of steel. He lets me feel a lump of steel and shows off a complicated-looking machine.

"You can make a cassette from a single, solid piece of steel, instead of punching the teeth one-by-one out of steel discs. Much better. Much easier."

And much more expensive, I think, because I know that the cassettes in 4130 chromoly steel he's talking about cost quite a lot. But I like the man, his workshop and the idea that a couple of floors below the espresso-drinking marketing men, there's a brain anticipating the next challenge the company will face. A new way of gear changing, a new way to soften a fork, a new way to make a cassette.

Not far from SRAM, there's a row of bikes for hire of the type now available in every big city driven by a new environmental philosophy. I'm looking at which gears they're equipped with – Shimano. It's hard to be a prophet in your own town.

STEEL Reynolds Technology is located in a small suburb of Birmingham, England. I step off the commuter train at Spring Road Station and continue to Shaftmoor Lane. Building 21 is dwarfed next to the much larger aircraft engine manufacturer Aero Engine Controls nearby. But that doesn't surprise me – Keith Noronha, with whom I spoke before our meeting, had said sadly: "There are fewer of us now. Far, far fewer." However, Reynolds' very existence means that an English factory that manufactures steel tubes for bicycles still exists, so I feel positive about it. But I will freely admit that this feeling is primarily one of nostalgia. In fact, it doesn't really matter in which country the steel pipes are manufactured.

Reynolds is primarily one of those brands that buyers and sellers of used bikes mention when they want to draw attention to the old-fashioned quality of their bike, the way things used to be done, things made in a reliable brick factory in England and not in a suspicious shed on the other side of the world. The same way the aircraft engine manufacturer on the other side of the big fence proudly proclaims that it is part of the Rolls-Royce Group. It sounds good, but doesn't have any real significance.

Being a brand familiar to all cyclists is of course an advantage, but in terms of Reynolds, it may also be a disadvantage, because most people think of their product as something that once existed but has since been replaced. Like those trying to sell ski clothing in natural materials – they're faced with skepticism by the

generation who believes they need to wear manmade garments to survive on the mountain and that woollen outfits belong to old documentary films where jaunty fitness enthusiasts rush around on birch skis and get their energy from raisins instead of energy bars.

So, when Keith Noronha shows me into a conference room with a lot of historical artifacts displayed, I wonder if he has the right idea. I know that he wants to present Reynolds as a modern steel component manufacturer but, despite that, the first thing he shows me is a patent letter from 1897 regarding butted tubing, an invention that helped reduce the weight of a frame by varying the thickness of the tubing walls. The tubes are thicker near the joints where they need the strength, and thinner elsewhere to save weight. This groundbreaking invention by Reynolds from the late 1800s should have been simple to achieve, I think, but it's not that easy. You have a smooth tube with walls of even thickness along its length. How do you get the tube walls thinner in some places and thicker in others while maintaining the outer dimension?

Keith Noronha explains that the process is based on a mould which shapes the inside of the tube. The mould is wider near the midsection of the tube and narrower at the ends. The mould is inserted into the tube and a machine presses the tube so that its internal dimensions follows the shape of the mould, while keeping its external profile even along its length. "Then," Keith says, almost triumphant, "the tube is rotated quickly to increase its width a little through centrifugal force. Otherwise, you wouldn't be able to remove the mould!"

I nod as if everything is obvious. However, this invention was revolutionary because a bicycle frame could be made much lighter, while retaining strength at the ends where it is needed.

We go into the factory. It's noisy, hissing, clattering, and smells of hot hydraulic oil and steel. To me, this is the essence of a factory as I remember it from my childhood when I accompanied my father, a mechanic, to work. It might say something about the lack of modernization at Reynolds.

Although Keith has explained the process, it's difficult to follow in reality. A frame tube is attached to the mouth of something that looks like a clamp on the end of a cylindrical lathe. A man pulls a lever and steps on a pedal, the tube enters the cylinder and is immediately spat back out again. The man then puts it in another pile. Pretty straightforward. As a spectator you see no difference. The tube has been reduced on the inside only. Keith shouts something about the fact that the finest tubes are made here in Birmingham. Others, of slightly lower quality, are made in Asia.

We go back into the conference room again because it's impossible to talk out in the factory. Keith explains that although Reynolds is most famous for its bicycle frames, they have always produced tubes for other things too: wheelchairs, aeroplanes, go-carts, Jaguar cars. Then he picks up some papers relating to the Reynolds 531, the tube that dominated the market for racing bikes for an unimaginably long period.

"Look here," Keith says, pointing to an old newspaper cutting. "Tour de France, 1964. In first place, Jacques Anquetil, the Frenchman known as 'Monsieur Chrono' for his outstanding ability to cycle against the clock. He rode on a Reynolds 531 frame. But you see, so did the rider who came in second place. And third, fourth and sixth place. And the women!"

Definitely impressive. But the most remarkable thing is that Reynolds 531 was an innovation from 1935. When Anquetil was crossing the finishing line on the Champs Elysées, he did it on an almost 30-year-old product. Indeed, over the years, there were a dozen different kinds of 531 tubes, but the base – a steel alloy with 1.5 percent manganese, 0.25 percent molybdenum and 0.35 percent carbon – was the same for more than 50 years before the Reynolds 653 was launched.

"Twenty-seven winners of the Tour de France have ridden on Reynolds frames," Keith continues. "All the greats: Eddy Merckx, Bernard Hinault and Miguel Indurain all won the tour on Reynolds."

Later, I read that the last time someone won the Tour on a steel frame was in 1994 – it was Miguel Indurain.

"But maybe we're on our way back up," Keith says, hopeful but with a tinge of desperation.

I'm having a hard time taking him seriously. Sure, there are a lot of enthusiasts who like steel frames for nostalgic reasons, and there are environmentally conscious cyclists who like steel because the material can be recycled. But everyone else who wants a light bike chooses aluminium or the even more popular carbon fibre. How will Reynolds win them back? As if Keith can read my thoughts, he says, "Steel is not really that heavy, even if that's what people think. It's because many people associate steel with bicycles for old people and because they've never experienced an exclusive steel racer."

Could it be that the steel went out of fashion more because of the current zeitgeist than because other materials had better qualities? Can it be that we can only picture steel as heavy and therefore we switched to bicycles made from one modern, supposedly magical material after another, even if we were only pedalling back and forth to the shops? Has steel became thought of in the same way that wool and leather is among outdoor people, something that only older people still use, while modern people move on to waterproof materials that are said to be breathable?

Keith sets out some promotional brochures for the British pro cycling team Madison Genesis.

"Their bike frames use Reynolds 953. A fantastic alloy! We can make strong tubes just 0.3mm thick. Madison Genesis has won a number of stages on steel frames. Twenty years after the material disappeared from the professional cycling world."

When I get home from Birmingham, I go to the garage and get out my two racing bikes, one with a modern carbon fibre frame and the other a retro bike in steel. I've always considered one to be lighter and more sensible, and the other to be heavier but more beautiful. They have equivalent wheels and the same set of gears. When I now weigh the bikes for the first time, there's only 108g (3¾oz) between them. A little while later, I receive a press release from British bicycle manufacturer Sven, announcing that they built an all-steel racer weighing just 6.3kg (13¾lb).

STYLE GUIDE What is it about cycling that makes everyone seem to have an aesthetic opinion about it? Outsiders ridicule us (men) as MAMILs (*see* "Lycra"), but even within the cycling world opinions are unabashed.

"You should wear your glasses on the outside of your helmet," said a complete stranger on my first club outing.

"What for?" I replied, too perplexed to say instead, "Mind your own business."

"That's just how people wear them. It's cooler."

"But then I have to take off the glasses every time I take off the helmet."

"Yeah, so what?"

Even more peculiar was an incident that happened when I went to buy a new saddlebag. I was going cycling in Spain and needed to carry a little more stuff than usual because I wouldn't be able to call anyone to come and help me if I needed it.

"But," the salesman said after showing me different models of saddlebags, "do you really want it on a racer? It's not really good for that."

"Really?" I replied, thinking that it would fit just fine.

"It will look ugly."

"Ugly?"

"Yeah, the style police, you know." Then he briefly told me what to put in my back pockets and how to pack them. "You can attach your spare tube under the saddle. It looks okay."

Of course, someone has written down all these rules and published them on the Velominati website under the title "The Rules." There are 95 rules listed. They include:

➻ Saddles, bars and tyres shall be carefully matched.
➻ Shorts should be black.

- Team kit is for members of the team only.
- Speeds and distances shall be referred to and measured in kilometres.
- Shorts and socks should be like Goldilocks. Not too long and not too short. No socks is a no-no, as are those ankle-length ones that should only be worn by female tennis players.
- No frame-mounted pumps.
- Humps are for camels: no hydration packs.
- Shave your guns. Legs are to be carefully shaved at all times.
- Tyres should be mounted so that the logo ends up next to the valve.
- Drink in moderation. Water bottles should be 500–610ml (17–21fl oz) maximum.
- Espresso or macchiato only – soy milk or skimmed milk is a no-no.
- One step from the bike and the helmet is off. Same thing for bicycle caps.
- No stickers on your bike, at all.
- Ditch the washer-nut and valve-stem cap. Mirrors should not be fitted either.
- Really small speedometers only. Power meters, heart-rate monitors and GPS are bulky, ugly and superfluous.
- No food on training rides under four hours.
- Never get out of the big ring. Only use the small gears when the slope is steeper than 20 percent.
- Descents are not for recovery.

Although this humourous advice is written tongue-in-cheek, I think there is a rule brigade out there who are hard to ignore. However, nowadays, at least if I'm cycling around Andalucía, I do it in mountain bike shoes, whose soles allow me to get off the bike and walk around if I want to explore a beautiful city. I have baggy mountain bike shorts because I want to look less like a MAMIL. I don't shave my legs either. And next time, I WILL buy a saddle bag. Or maybe not; they're actually quite ugly.

TANDEM Sure, it's a little faster, but otherwise, what's the point? It makes me think of the back of a pantomime horse when I see someone on the back of a tandem. They can't see anything and have their nose pressed up against their fellow rider's sweaty back. It must be the cycling equivalent of drawing the short straw.

If it wasn't for the slightly increased speed of riding a tandem, I would think that the invention had only come about so a man could keep track of his wife. Indeed, many strange inventions from cycling's distant past were related to this. Tales of three-wheelers and four-wheelers so that women could ride in their long dresses, and bicycles with two seats side by side so amorous couples could ride together.

If a man's wish for control of his wife was behind the invention of the tandem bicycle, I would have thought that their marital relationship would rather quickly be put to the test. This is because the one at the front always believes that the one behind is not pedalling enough, and vice versa. Riding a tandem is – like paddling a canoe or playing croquet – something you should avoid doing as a new couple.

Tandem actually existed as an Olympic sport until the 1972 Munich Games. After that, the sport was done away with, thank goodness.

"TATTOOS with a bicycle motif; do you do a lot of those?" asked my youngest daughter when she got a small turtle tattooed on her shoulder blade.

"Bikes? Yes, God yes, all the time," replied the tattooist.

He's certainly right. A quick search online results in multiple hits: a cycling frog, a skull with a bicycle helmet, a bicycle chain snake, gears, stylized bikes in all forms and smart mottos such as "Ride to live – Live to ride" and "LOVE – VELO." There are also clever things in Latin you have to go home and look up, such as "*vivendum est equitare*", which means "living is cycling", though "*equitare*" really means "riding". They didn't have bikes in the ancient world.

TIGHT CLOTHING is worn by cyclists for three main reasons:

1. Because it's comfortable.
2. Because it reduces air resistance.
3. So they can ridicule any cyclists who believe that cycling clothes should be the same as walking clothes because it is basically the same idea.

TILLIE ANDERSON, whose nickname was Tillie the Terrible Swede, was the world's best female cyclist in the late 19th century. Or at least if your world was Chicago, which was where Tillie lived.

Since I happen to be in Chicago, I'm going to The Swedish American Museum to see what they have about Tillie, this undeniably unique Swedish-American cult hero. They have nothing, it turns out.

"I think there's a children's book in the store," says the woman at the desk.

There *is* a children's book. Sue Stauffacher has written *Tillie the Terrible Swede – How One Woman, a Sewing Needle, and a Bicycle Changed History*. I flick through Stauffacher's book. She's chosen to make it a feel-good story on the theme of even-girls-can-achieve-if-they-put-their-minds-to-it-and-fight-on. That's only half the story of Tillie Anderson.

Tillie was at the top of her game. She held the record for both sprint and long distance, as well as being the reigning World Champion, when the League of American Bicyclists banned female race cyclists in 1902. That same year, her husband and coach, Filip, died from tuberculosis. A few years earlier, in

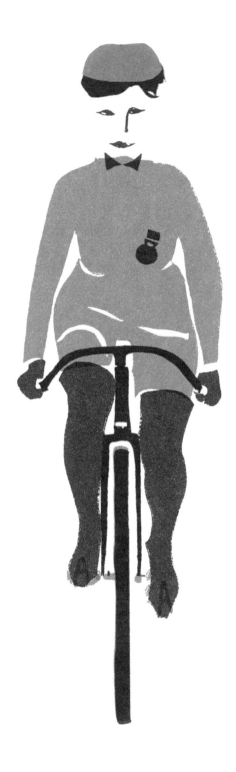

1894, the same organization had banned non-white cyclists, a rule that remained in place until 1999. The ban on female cyclists was based on the usual male fears of strong women and a vision of a future society in which it was not obvious that men would be in charge. The arguments put forward were partly that a female athlete's grimace during cycling, known as the "bike face", could be permanent and that the woman's body could be deformed and lose its ability to give birth to children. In addition, the organization considered that it was profoundly immoral that men could pay to see women riding in a velodrome in tight-fitting outfits.

In order to investigate the allegations of physical deformation, Tillie was examined by a group of doctors. Their conclusions, along with drawings of Tillie's legs, were published, according to Stauffacher, in a daily newspaper: "Although Miss Anderson's limbs are not as regular from an artistic point of view, her general health is better [...] Simply put, from head to foot, she is a mass of muscle."

Despite the fact that Tillie was excluded from competitions, she continued to be faithful to the sport and, in 2000, she was posthumously inducted into the United States Bicycling Hall of Fame.

TITANIUM is an almost magic material. It doesn't rust, it tolerates acids very well, has high heat resistance, is stronger than steel, harder than steel, and isn't rejected by the human body, which is why it's used for prostheses and dental work. The British company Enigma still builds titanium bikes.

Although titanium is the ninth most common element in the Earth's crust, it's expensive to process and, moreover, more difficult to weld and drill than steel. It was therefore a long while before bicycle frames were built from titanium and when they finally were, it coincided with the next generation of carbon fibre. There are those who claim, in a very conspiratorial fashion, that titanium is even better than carbon fibre. The fact that carbon fibre now completely dominates the cycling world at competition level, these people will say, is solely the result of marketing (misleading marketing) and cheaper production costs – you pour oil into one end of a machine in Taiwan and get a carbon fibre frame out of the other end.

Today, when frame manufacturers market titanium, they extol the strength, lightness and rust-resistance of the material. They also put forward the argument that a titanium frame doesn't break in a crash, which aluminium and carbon fibre frames do. In addition, there's the point that titanium frames, almost magically, are more forgiving to the cyclist in terms of vibration.

Today, titanium frames are bought mostly by people who want to distance themselves from anonymous Asian plastics and want to emphasize that they are not nostalgic steel enthusiasts. For them, titanium is the material of the future, whose future was stolen by carbon fibre. Plus most of today's titanium bikes are stunningly beautiful.

A TOURING BICYCLE is a type of bike designed for long journeys. It's built to carry heavy loads, has plenty of low gears and the ability to hang panniers down low, both front and rear, for a better centre of gravity. The idea is to be able to bring everything with you on your trip, because of course it isn't even remotely possible to buy supplies once you leave the comforts of your home town.

It's a bicycle bought by those with big plans, such as cycling to China, around Tasmania, or pedalling the length of the American coast. These bikes are often resold after six months due to "sudden injury".

THE TRAILER that we attached behind the bike is something we got when our daughters were small. I rode with them to kindergarten, dropping off both the children and the trailer, and then continued on my way to work. In the evening, the reverse procedure.

But, if I'm honest, I never really liked the trailer. Firstly, it didn't seem safe to be towing them behind me. I know this was mostly just a personal feeling, but I never could shake it off. Secondly, I couldn't talk to them during the journey when they sat behind me, usually under a plastic cover. The little chats I liked to have with them when I dropped them off and picked them up from kindergarten became impossible.

In retrospect, I feel I should have chosen a cargo bike instead. Then I could have communicated with the children during the journey and kept my eye on them. The disadvantage would have been that I would then have had to commute to work on a cargo bike, but it would have been worth the sacrifice.

THE TRIALS BIKE is perhaps the strangest bicycle of them all because, in most cases, it lacks a saddle. The trials bike is part of the mountain bike family but has fairly few similarities to a mountain bike because it doesn't have suspension, gears and, as already mentioned, a saddle. A trials bike has wide rims, low tyre pressure and, with the right rider, can tackle most obstacles and avoid getting into trouble.

A mountain bike trial is a race in which the competitors aim to complete a course in the shortest time and, preferably, without putting a foot on the ground, something they are penalized for. The course is either a natural one with stony paths, rocks and other obstacles, or in a city with park benches, steps, walls and other manmade obstacles.

The sport is thought to have been invented by the father of Catalan motorcycle trials rider Ot Pi. In Barcelona the sport is called *El bicitrial*. Ot's father, Pere Pi, built the first trials bike when Ot was six years old so he could practice for motorcycle trials on an ordinary bike. The bike was the first model to be made by the bicycle brand Monty.

A TUBULAR TYRE (also known as a sew-up) takes 32 seconds to sew together. Sometimes a few more, sometimes a few less. I have, like other people interested in time and motion, timed the woman at Continental's tyre factory in Korbach, who sits at a powerful sewing machine with the vertical needle pattering away.

A tubular tyre is most simply described as a tyre that is sewn around a regular inner tube. The strange thing about tubular tyres is that they continue to exist, even in professional circles, even though they're no longer any better than the clincher tyres with a separate inner tube. Yes, they may be a tad lighter, they can run with a greater variety of tyre pressures and, in case of a high-speed puncture, they have a greater inclination to stay on the rim. But if I had to guess, it's mainly three things that help keep the tubular tyre going: when a professional gets a puncture, a serviceman arrives immediately with a new wheel; the professional doesn't have to spend half the night trying to glue a new one; and the pro doesn't have to pay for the new tubing out of his own pocket.

"How much of your production is tubular tyres?" I ask Continental's production manager.

"About three percent."

The woman has now finished sewing the new tyre. Thirty-two seconds have passed. Every time she's forced to fiddle with the valve, otherwise it would have been faster. The tubular tyre that the woman has sewn will cost quite a bit to buy, which is justified by the argument that they're handmade in Germany. I myself have one. They were on a bike I bought online. But I've found an old book that shows how to repair a punctured tubular tyre. You untack the seam, poke out the tube, repair it in the usual way, poke it back in and sew it together again. Repairing it requires: patch, solution, sandpaper, twine, needle, thimble, ballpoint pen and talcum powder. Plus, infinitely more time than 32 seconds.

THE TYRE FACTORY is in Korbach, in Germany. Throughout my visit to Continental's huge facility, no one has managed to explain why it's located there. It's nice, hilly farmland, but in the middle of nowhere. Of course, no place in Germany is sparsely populated, but it's as though the major cities of Kassel, Frankfurt, Bonn, Cologne, Düsseldorf and Dortmund had drawn a circle in the landscape and decided that inside the circle, there wouldn't be much there. Except for Continental's tyre factory, because it's always been there.

I've been allowed to join a tour put on for a group of foreign bicycle dealers who will be shown around and buttered-up just enough that it doesn't count as a bribe according to the European Commission. Later, they will get to drive a racing car, but those cars, of course, also have tyres, and bicycle dealers sell tyres.

The dealers and I pass some offices and enter a gate into the actual factory buildings, some of which date from the early 20th century.

"Everything," says Marco Buhl, our guide, "began in Hanover in 1871 when the Continental-Caoutchouc und Gutta-Percha Compagnie was founded."

"Three thousand people work here in Korbach," Marco continues. "In other locations a long way away, others are also working on bicycle tyres. In the group as a whole, we are closer to hundreds of thousands of people."

The plan for Marco's tour is to emphasize to us that the bicycle tyres made in Germany are made with far greater craftsmanship than those made more cheaply elsewhere, even in Continental's own factories in China. There should be a quality difference; better material and higher puncture protection, which should also be reflected in the price. Each tyre should earn its label "Made in Germany".

To mark this difference, the German tyres have slightly cooler names, such as "Black Chili" and "Gatorskin", while the tyres from China are called "Safety" or "Plus".

"All the rubber is mixed here in the factory. In bicycle tyres, there is a lot of natural rubber, latex."

"Is there an eco label?" I wonder as someone who has, for a while, been purchasing ecolabelled car tyres without HA oils (high aromatic oils), which are carcinogenic.

Marco squirms a bit before he answers.

"No, not yet, but we are working on it. There is a market."

Now we're standing in front of a machine manufacturing clincher tyres – the most common type, where two enclosed steel wires keep the tyre in place in the rim. I realize it's a rather complicated process.

First, up to eight different kinds of natural and synthetic rubbers (plus some chemicals and pigments) are combined to get the right mix for this particular tyre. Then the rubber is rolled through different machines to get the correct width and thickness. Next, a woman at a machine tears off a piece of rubber along a perforated line and puts it around a drum she can rotate with a pedal. Then she adds layer upon layer, a tread, a puncture guard and then the two steel rings, and finally the edge wire itself.

I count 15 different steps, including those that involve cutting with scissors and smoothing the rubber layers by hand. Undoubtedly, the work needs to be done by hand and by someone with knowledge and experience, but would I call it craftsmanship? No. Possibly "handmade", but I'm doubtful. The woman at the machine is just another machine, but capable of learning things. In any case, to consider something as craftsmanship, the person making it should bring something personally to the work. As if there would be no product without the input of the person making it. But I could be wrong.

We continue on to the next step in the process, which is vulcanization. This is a magical process where the material is transformed; it gains another property by adding heat. The rubber goes from being plastic to being elastic. Don't ask me to explain it. It has something to do with how the molecules are arranged. Before the vulcanization, you can pull the tyre into whatever shape you want. After the vulcanization, the tyre always returns to its original form. That's why you can't make new tyres out of old rubber. It's not possible to melt old car tyres so instead they are granulated and used, for example, as a resilient surface under an artificial lawn.

A while back I went to Gislaved Industrial Museum and saw their rubber and tyre exhibition. Now, in Korbach, I find that so much of tyre production is still the same. If a worker from the 1870s Continental-Caoutchouc and Gutta-Percha Compagnie was resurrected and could step through these doors, it would all look familiar. He would be surprised that all the power and heat comes from electricity through magic cables, but otherwise, *kein Problem*. After a brief update, he could start working.

I ask how long it takes to make a tyre if you add up all the stages. I'm not trying to make a point, I pose the question out of wonder. Because when human labour is involved for more than a minute in producing something, production usually ends up in a country with low wage costs.

"Don't actually know," replies Marco.

To me, it's clear that he knows. Perhaps he doesn't want to reveal how few minutes it really takes. We who pay a lot for a tyre handmade in Germany may be a little disappointed if it only takes five minutes, or maybe fifteen if you include packaging and transport.

Even though production techniques haven't changed much, there's been a lot of progress when it comes to tyres. Today, they're so much lighter than before. The puncture protection is excellent and even a chunky mountain bike tyre with deep treads can now be folded and carried in your back pocket.

Next, we listen to Marco's boss tell some stories – many of them small gripes about manufacturing. Mostly bad feeling that dates back to at least 1926 when the French manufacturer Mavic introduced aluminium wheels. Suddenly, tyre manufacturers had to adapt to these new wheels and they did not like it. They wanted – and still want – to drive development themselves and not have to adapt to others' innovations. In 1926, the fear was that aluminium wheels would become too hot and thereby cause punctures, which was why they were banned in the Tour de France until 1931. This attitude is still there when the boss talks about carbon fibre wheels.

"The risk is that they get too hot. Nice tyres contain a lot of natural rubber, latex, which has a melting point of $54\,°C$ ($129\,°F$). We have pointed this out to the wheel manufacturers, but they just shrug their shoulders and wait for all bikes to have disc brakes. Then the problem of overheated wheels disappears. But until then, it is we who get the blame when cyclists get punctures, even though it's unfair."

ULTRACYCLING is a type of cycling for those who think that gruelling Tours are just too short. Roughly speaking, there are two kinds of races: those with a set time, and those with a set distance. Common to both is the fact that the clock keeps running even when you take a break or sleep.

An example of a time-limited race is the Melfar 24, which takes place in Middelfart, Denmark, each year and, as the name suggests, runs for 24 hours. During that time, the riders have to complete as many laps of the three courses as possible. They start in the morning on the day course which is 56km (35 miles) round, then move on to the night course as it gets dark, which is 15km (9½ miles). The last hour of cycling takes place on a track of just under 3km (about 2 miles). The rider who has completed the most laps wins.

The most famous ultrarace, where distance is the goal, is the RAAM or Race Across America. The route for this race has varied slightly over the years, but it always starts somewhere on the West Coast and ends somewhere on the East Coast, a distance of around 4,800km (3,000 miles). The best cyclists manage to cross the American continent in around eight days, including rests and sleep time.

The Tour d'Afrique is even further at around 12,000km (7,456 miles) and runs between Cairo and Cape Town: about one hundred days of pedalling, plus twenty rest days. It's run by TDA Global Cycling, who are based in Toronto. They also do the Orient Express (Paris–Istanbul) and Silk Route (Istanbul–Beijing).

THE UNICYCLE is a type of wheeled transport previously only seen in the circus. No longer just in the circus ring, however, the unicycle can now be found in the most unexpected places. You won't believe it until you see with your own eyes just how many versions of the unicycle there now are: flatland, racing, street, trials, commuting and the muni – where the M stands for "mountain," – which includes further variations of cross country, offroad and downhill. There is, of course, still a circus version. There are unicycles with disc brakes and those with gears. Very tall unicycles are called giraffes.

In addition, there are clubs for unicycle enthusiasts who organize competitions, ranging from 100m (328ft) races and marathons, to high jump events, technical course races and mountain bike races. Teams of unicyclists also compete at handball, basketball and a type of indoor hockey.

THE VELODROME is a beautiful oval of gleaming parquet and steeply banked curves. Nice, but when you're in it on a bike you're not used to, the facility's aesthetic values aren't exactly the first thing you think about.

"Now we're going to ride harder! Increase the speed," says Göran, who is running the introductory course.

And I'm riding harder. Increasing my speed. Going as fast as I can. I look up and it looks just as horrible as I feared. I'm on a high-speed bike headed straight for a wall. At least that's what it feels like. This isn't how I thought it would be. It didn't look like this when I was in London and got the idea that I might try riding in a velodrome.

It was early April in Herne Hill: wisteria, cherry blossom and bright green grass. Twenty-two cyclists gather. Mostly men but a few women. This part of south London is lovely – posh and extremely exclusive. It borders Brixton, the Brixton of race riots and punk songs. The velodrome in Herne Hill was built in 1891 and hosted cycling events for the Olympics in 1948.

I watch the cyclists riding at a lap time of 40 seconds. It looks pretty easy as they go round the 450m (492 yard) concrete track. The curves aren't very steep either, at only 30 percent. It's like a shallow concrete bowl.

But it looks nice. Spinning before spinning classes, spinning without music, spinning outdoors in the sunshine. The cyclists ride round in pairs or clusters. On the far bend the main pair drift higher up using centrifugal force. It seems like they're treading water when the group slides past below them, or as if they're floating like falcons over their prey. Then they dive down to their new positions all the way in the rear. They're going a bit faster now, 36 seconds per lap. On the inside of the main track, groups of school children of different sizes compete, wearing cycle tops with sponsors' logos.

Velodromes were first constructed in various places around the world in the second half of the 19th century. The reasons were two-fold. Firstly, roads were mostly in poor condition and dangerous for cyclists, and secondly because it was easier to charge an entrance fee if the audience came to a velodrome than if they just stood watching the cycling along a country road. The last major velodrome to be built was the one in Turkmenistan's capital Ashgabat, with stands that accommodate six thousand people.

Velodrome cycling has always been pretty big in Britain and many of their best road cyclists come from there. For example, Mark Cavendish has a World Cup gold medal and Sir Bradley Wiggins has seven Olympic medals. Wiggins, by the way, began his career right here in Herne Hill.

Velodrome cycling was an event in the Olympic Games in 1896, though it wasn't until 1988 that it was added as a women's sport. The first and only time it was not included in the Olympic program was in 1912 when the Olympic Games were held in Stockholm. Why, I do not know.

In velodrome cycling, there are three different racing categories with a total of ten different branches. The simplest sprint races involve riding as fast as possible, individually or in packs, with a stationary or rolling start. There's also an untimed sprint, won by the first rider to complete a certain number of laps. Two riders start at the same time and the winner must be both cunning and fast. Because there is an advantage to hanging back behind your competitor at the final stage of the race, there will be a lot of racing games, slow cycling, even waiting stationary (track standing) before the final finish is decided.

Then there are pursuit races – both individual and team races – where you start on opposite sides of the velodrome and the aim is to catch your opponent.

A Madison is a kind of relay event with teams of two or three riders, only one of each team riding at a time, usually for 25–50km (15½–31 miles). There's a variation of this called a six-day race in which the teams cycle round the clock for six days and those who travel the furthest win. The current world record was set by the German riders Huschke and Krupkat who, in Berlin in 1924, managed 4,544km (2,824 miles) with an average speed of 31.6kph (19.6mph). In the past, if none of the riders was trying to set a world record, these six-day events became fairly relaxed affairs. At the times of the day when spectators were few and far between, the cyclists took it easy. They kept an eye on their positions in the race, but could be seen reading a newspaper or writing a letter as they cycled around, and around, and around.

Today, as most events are much shorter, the goal is no longer to cycle the furthest, but to collect points along the way. The spectators generally consume large quantities of beer. In Munich, there's a theme park around the velodrome and a nightclub in the basement that opens as the cyclists finish for the day.

"So, you've never ridden a fixie?" Göran asked.

"Nope."

"Okay. This bike: it has no brakes, it has no gears, it has no freewheel."

"Why?"

"It goes really fast. If there were brakes and you slowed down, people would crash into you. Most bikes don't even have a speedometer, because one look at it is enough for you to lose concentration and cause a crash."

We're getting started. Initially, it's slow. A 48-tooth chainring on the front and a 15-tooth sprocket behind is for achieving high speeds. There is a woman in the group who hasn't cycled a velodrome bike before and is as nervous as I am, but seems to be more anxious. We start pedalling. I hang in there. I don't want to be the worst. First we're on the flat bit, then we ride up the banking a bit and ride on the blue mark called the Côte d'Azur, the French Riviera. We ride a few laps. Pause for new instructions. Hands on the frame. Then we ride higher up. It's not any harder higher up, there's just further to fall. If you fall off, it's usually because you're riding too slowly. The centrifugal force becomes too low, gravity overcomes friction and the rear wheel slides.

We do a few more laps, then Göran leads us upwards and upwards and soon we're at the top where the advertisements end and, if I dare looked down, I might have vertigo. But I don't

look down. I relax, realize that the bike steers itself through the bends, that I can achieve a better line if I sit heavy and let the bike choose its path. It's an amazing rush when you go for it and push through the bend and come out on other side.

"It is addictive," says Göran.

Finally, we are doing a rolling start. We take a lap to warm up, then cycle for three laps, and the final lap is timed.

"When you come out of the last bend on the second lap, you should be at the top and then descend to the starting line. Take advantage of the slope, then take the corner as far down as possible where it's shortest."

I'm out first. Three laps, I think, how hard can it be? It can be incredibly hard. By the time the bell rings, I'm already really tired and my thigh muscles are burning. But I'm high up on the track, which allows me to descend to the starting line and aim to take the corner as low as possible. Somewhere I lose my nerve. I don't dare push myself any faster. But around I come, dash down the straight and come into the final corner at such a speed that I'll need a lap just to slow down. Then it's the turn of the woman I noticed earlier. She doesn't seem to be going as fast as I was, but she takes the corners in a nicer way, more smoothly where I felt I was swerving. However, my observation appears to be correct. I beat her – by one-hundredth of a second.

THE VÉLODROME D'HIVER is an horrific, tragic exception to the usually good associations that cycling brings. This velodrome – built in 1909 and torn down in 1959 – was used in July 1942 by the German occupation and the French Vichy regime to hold Paris' Jews as they awaited deportation.

Over eight thousand Jews – men, women and children – were held for five days under heinous conditions: no food, no water, barely any sanitary facilities. Thereafter, children were separated from adults, and they were all were sent to Auschwitz and other extermination camps. French nationals were involved in this incident, but no French were ever charged with ethnic cleansing and, for a long time, France officially downplayed its involvement in the deportation of Jews – even denied it.

Today, there is a memorial to those held at the velodrome on the Quai de Grenelle. It takes six minutes to cycle there from the Eiffel Tower.

THE VIBRATIONS began affecting me about six months after I started cycling more regularly. I started having trouble with my feet going numb. At first, I thought it was due to the cold winter weather and my cold plastic shoes that didn't retain heat even if I had shoe covers on, but when spring came, the trouble didn't go away. Rather, my feet became increasingly numb and by now it was the middle of summer. It was 30°C (86°F) in Corsica but my fingers still began to lose feeling. By the end of a 30km (19 mile) ride, I had lost the feeling in two of my fingers and it didn't return for several weeks.

By now, I started to think I might be ill. I went online and Googled for information about numb extremities. It was a bad idea because there's a plethora of scary disorders that start with numb fingers and toes. So I managed to get a referral to a neurologist for some tests. After extensive testing, the doctor pronounced me to be completely healthy.

"But my toes and fingers go numb when I ride a bike."

"Choose a different sport, then."

I managed to stop myself from saying, "But I've invested vast amounts of money in my bikes."

Since the tests, I've tried softer soles in my shoes, more shock-resistant handlebar tape, gloves with more gel, wider and less inflated tyres. Nothing has helped. On the bright side, I often forget I've lost feeling in my extremities, and it tends to come back immediately I get off the bike. So, there isn't really much to complain about.

The neurologist was checking, I think, to see if I was suffering from Carpal Tunnel Syndrome (not MS, as I feared). The symptoms are just numbness in the fingers, but usually also a burning pain. The reason is that a nerve in the wrist is being trapped. This syndrome can have a variety of causes, ranging from diabetes and pregnancy, to holding onto vibrating handlebars for too long. It's treated with rest, handlebar tape and, in severe cases, surgery.

VULTURES are what cyclists call people who have a macabre desire to stand at the place on the course where a crash is most likely to occur.

A WATT is a unit of power. For example, a vacuum cleaner can draw anything from 500 to 2,000 watts. The amount that appears on your electricity bill depends on how long you use your vacuum cleaner. The amount is usually expressed in kilowatt-hours, that is, how many thousands of watts it uses in an hour.

Many aspects of cycling can be calculated in watts. On the one hand, it's about you, the cyclist, and how many watts you can generate to power your bicycle. On the other hand, it's about the power that is slowing you down such as friction and air resistance, which must be minimized to achieve good speed and efficiency.

If you rode your bike in space without the effects of gravity and wind resistance (don't laugh – in early space stations there were bicycle tracks similar to a hamster wheel to keep the astronauts trim), it would be easy to measure your energy output over a certain distance. To calculate how much energy you have expended, all you need to know is your weight and that of your bike, how far you've travelled and how fast you went. On Earth, however, a lot of different factors come into play: the wind, the road, the bike, how hilly it is and if you shaved your legs. And a lot more. So of course there is a plethora of gadgets to measure your output. They can tell you when you're performing poorly and if you should practise more.

A power meter can sit in the rear wheel, in the crank or in the pedals, and it can not only measure if you will struggle uphill, but even if you are applying your power inefficiently. There are also special exercise bikes that measure the effort you are putting in in terms of the energy you are generating. A common feature of all of these is their hefty price. The same is true of aerodynamic bikes – each watt saved in air resistance costs a handsome sum.

To invest as an amateur in a power meter feels a bit like overkill. On the other hand, it can be fun to know how well you are performing and how your power output changes round a course. If you're in a good club, there might be equipment or a Wattbike you can borrow. Which is quite sufficient.

When you're calculating wattage, there are two things that are fun to note. The first is that a human is a rather inefficient machine. Somewhere I read that a really good velodrome cyclist can expend 2,000 watts over two laps of the track. That's only enough energy to vacuum a door mat. A really good professional racing cyclist can, on average, reach just under 500 watts and would need to ride for about 14 hours to generate the energy required for the hot shower he takes after finishing the race.

It's also amusing to compare how well a bicycle compares to other modes of transport. On average, a cyclist needs to generate about 16 watt-hours to move the bicycle 1km (0.6 mile). The following figures show how much energy is required to move a person 1km by:

➼ walking: 41.6 watt-hours (2.6 times as much as cycling)
➼ tram: 243.2 watt-hours (15.2 times as much)
➼ car: 560 watt-hours (35 times as much)
➼ aeroplane: 644.8 watt-hours (40.3 times as much)

THE WEIGHT of a competition bike must not be less than 6.8kg (15lb).
The rule was set in 2000, partly so that manufacturers wouldn't undermine safety in their efforts to produce lighter and lighter bikes, and partly so that everyone could compete on the same terms.

Today, many of the best bikes weigh less than 6.8kg (15lb) and mechanics tape fishing weights to the bikes to reach the qualifying weight in competitions. The lightest, fully functional racing bike I have ever come across weighs 2.72kg (6lb).

THE WHEEL HUB DYNAMO It wasn't until the invention of the
LED lamp that the hub dynamo truly became useful. Previously, the dynamo was usually mounted on the front or rear fork and its head was angled down, rolling against the edge of the tyre. It was never really satisfactory as it required a lot of power, worked poorly when wet, and could cause a catastrophic crash if a screw came loose and the dynamo ended up in the spokes. However,

there wasn't really anywhere else to put it and only the high speed of the rotating outer edge of the wheel could generate enough electricity to power the light bulbs of the time.

The hub rotates, of course, as many turns as the tyre does, but its speed is considerably lower. But since an LED lamp may only require five percent of the power needed to light up an old-fashioned light bulb, the hub's relatively slow rotation is sufficient to provide enough light.

WHITE BICYCLES There's a series of well-known photographs of John Lennon and Yoko Ono at the Hilton Hotel in Amsterdam. The year is 1969, the world-famous couple had just got married and were spending their honeymoon in bed as a protest against the Vietnam War. The bedlinen is white, their robes are white, in the room are white flowers and a white dove in a white cage. Stuck to the window behind the bed are two hand-drawn posters with the words "Hair peace" and "Bed peace". Another feature that appears in many of the pictures is a white bicycle decorated with red and yellow flowers. The bike is at the foot of the bed and, at first glance, looks more like a piece of modern art than a working bicycle – both the chain and the wheels are coloured white. But the white bike is believed to have been used many times by many people.

This *witte fiets*, as the white bike was called in Dutch, was part of the Provo protest movement. The name came from the word "provocation" and the idea was to provoke a violent response from the authorities with peaceful actions. The group's activities were divided into different actions, each with the prefix "white". Chimneys were painted white to highlight harmful emissions, there was a women's plan that was white and was about sexual education, a white house plan to draw attention to property speculation, and a children's plan, which included a kind of cooperative kindergarten. In addition, there was a white car plan with the purpose of setting up a car pool with small electric cars. And there was the white bike plan, which was perhaps the world's first system of cycle hires. Lost and found bicycles were renovated, painted white and left around Amsterdam for anyone to borrow. The seemingly random white bicycle in the newlyweds' bedroom was actually a deliberate act of protest against motoring and capitalism.

The British psychedelic rock band Tomorrow made a song about the phenomenon, and *My White Bicycle* later became a big hit when supergroup Nazareth covered it.

WINE CYCLING

I fill my water bottles at the fountain on the square in Bédoin – just one of those things people do – and I head out of town, vineyards on either side of the road. Heavy, violet-blue clusters of fruit hang off the vines almost down to the ground and appear to be ready for picking. These vines aren't exactly beautiful when they're cultivated so intensely. Rows of thick, waist-high stumps with a few fluffy leaves and a handful of bunches of fruit on each. Rows that make the landscape look like a bad comb-over. The olive groves and patches of citrus trees dotted between the vineyards are certainly more beautiful.

It's a good time to ride a bike in this part of Provence. The first week of September and most of the French have gone home after their holidays, but it's still warm and the hotels and restaurants haven't started to close up for the winter yet.

I pass Crillon-le-Brave, the brave Crillon – wasn't that a character in a novel? The landscape opens up, and each village is perched on a small hill that I have to pedal up and over. The air is clear and clean. I stop in Caromb for a coffee. In the square, there is a market. Old ladies squeeze melons, inspect tomatoes and sniff *saucissons*. Fresh fish and blueberry liqueur are sold here. Someone is buying a hot cooked chicken from a mobile rotisserie, someone else is buying eggs in bulk and carefully carrying them home. Tourists stroll around, and groups of walkers are passing by in hefty boots as they go to join up with the GR911, one of France's many hiking routes.

Out of Caromb, the Mistral wind buffets my ears. I hunker down and lean into the gusts and think that the good news is that this particular wind never blows for more than three days at a time. The bad news is that my entire ride only lasts three days.

I take a break in Gigondas to taste some wine. I tell the woman behind the counter that the region was recommended by a friend who thought Gigondas was the best wine around. That makes her so happy, she claps her hands.

I'm not very good at tasting wine. It takes intense things to wake my taste buds. Bold and oaky are my wines of choice. Fruity and elegant are qualities I really dislike. All white wines taste the same to me – almost.

"The grapes will be harvested in a week," says the woman. "But the harvest celebrations already started two days ago. The days of spontaneous celebrations are long gone. Nowadays a band has to be booked, a stage rented, barbecue cooks hired and sales stands assembled. You must have the party first and the harvest later."

But if Gigondas is the best wine, which wine is second best? The woman looks at a map, and after a while says "Vinsobres."

"They also have the status of Rhône Cru, the highest category."

"Okay," I say, "then I'll cycle there," even though I realize it's about 25km (15½ miles) into the wind.

I stop in Séguret for lunch. A nice little town and one of the *Plus Beaux Villages de France*, the most beautiful villages in France. I find a restaurant with a view, though it's windy, and I order a Corsican salad because I'm always a sucker for the combination of delicate salad leaves and figatelli sausages. And

a glass of rosé to go with it. The view of the valley is nice, but now the wind is really picking up. My napkin floats away and the bread basket is blown off the table and continues along the ground like a small radio-controlled car.

"No, it does not contain celery," says the waitress to a neighbouring diner, while at the same time catching a huge parasol that lifts off the ground and threatens to fall on a table laden with three crème brûlées and a vanilla ice cream.

Continuing on my ride, I follow signs for cycle paths that turn off the road. I ride along very narrow paths through the vineyards. There I can smell the warm soil, hear the cicadas chirping and see birds of prey dive down from the sky like huge brown swallows on anabolic steroids. Usually, I have no idea where these cycle paths are taking me, but it doesn't matter.

They can't be that wrong.

I approach Vinsobres. I taste some wine in a rather charming place after which I start looking for somewhere to stay the night. I go into the tourist office, where a woman tells me that the bar opposite the church has rooms.

"But that's all I know," the woman continues, smiling. "It's a shame that the tourist office isn't open."

"But where am I, then?" I wonder, puzzled.

"This is the mayor's office."

The bar is closed. There's a large enamel sign on the door that says the place is closed on Wednesdays. Today is Tuesday.

Vinsobres. Doesn't it sound like the name of a wine that makes you sober? Or do I have my languages all mixed up? I consult my map. It's another 10km (6 miles) or so over a steep hill to the next town. And yes, it lies in the north, as well. Straight to the wind.

Most people who like the idea of wine cycling go on a package tour. When they arrive, the bikes are ready, the routes are fixed, the food bags are arranged in advance and they have their luggage transported to each pre-booked hotel. Right about now, I wish I had booked that kind of holiday. Instead, I just had the idea, asked a bicycle hire company if they had both a touring bike and a couple of panniers to rent, poured my luggage into them and pedalled off, just like that. Totally random. That's why I've now ended up in Valréas. On the one hand, the town is in a less-than-charming area of Provence, but on the other hand, the ordinariness is liberating in a way. There are young people hanging out in cafés, people in bars drinking wine without sniffing it first, not a single British hobbyist painting sunflowers, and a general pride in being France's main focus of the paper and cardboard industry. In addition, I find the Grand Hôtel – it's like something in a movie. I'm the only guest and the porter looks like Einstein.

"You can put your bicycle in the lounge, *pas de problème*. You can have a room overlooking the garden and the pool is over there – yes, under all those leaves. This wind, it's terrible."

Taking a cycling holiday among vineyards is now quite common. Most people who go on cycling package holidays either pedal along the Rhine, here in Provence or in Tuscany. The package includes bicycle hire, accommodation, luggage transport and in some cases, half or even full board. If you want to be a little more spontaneous, pack your things into two suitcases, fly to your destination, hire a bike on site and then pedal wherever you want and stay where you like. Try taking a flight to Palermo and cycling down the Sicilian west coast, or fly to Pisa and cycle along the coast to Rome or Milan to experience the classic Barolo–Barbaresco wine route, which is sometimes a stage in the Giro d'Italia. Or fly to Porto and cycle along the Douro River stopping at various port wine producers. Or around Rioja after taking the train from Barcelona. Or Corsica, or Provence starting in Marseilles.

It's hard to go wrong. Actually, nearly impossible. The biggest problem is the bicycle rental, but you just look around and soon you'll find a bicycle hire with someone who seems happy to help you. Nowadays, you can also rent electric bikes, which is great if someone travelling with you is a little less fit. Since everyone now books their accommodation on the internet, a somewhat strange phenomenon has arisen: there's usually a centrally located charming old hotel with rooms available because it doesn't have its own website.

The wine here in Valréas will have to wait. Instead, I find the fabulous Café de Paris where the charming owner plays jazz, accompanied by female singers, and serves me excellent *moules frites*, a gastronomic combination of mussels and French fries. The mussels are delicious and the French fries, I imagine, are just what a cyclist might need.

The next morning, Einstein serves breakfast and tells me that the wind has got worse.

"I have worked here at the Grand Hôtel for 42 years," he says, answering my question and finishing his sentence with a big sigh.

That's when I should have said that I'm sure he has made his guests happy all these years. The last thing he does is fill my water bottles.

"I put in some ice cubes, *bonne journée!*"

I cycle back the same way I came yesterday. Over the mountain and through Vinsobres. Next, I ride through the vineyards. Tractors plough and trim the top growth off the vines, probably so the plant's final burst of energy will be focused on the ripening grapes, not wasted on new shoots. The earth is stony and there doesn't seem to be a lot of room for soil, but obviously there's enough. Sometimes there is a rose bush planted at the end of each row of vines. In the Champagne region, a wine producer once told me that the roses were the equivalent of the miners' canary birds, since they warned the farmer of an acid deficiency in the soil. If the roses shrivelled, they knew at once that the soil had lost its acidity.

In Mirabel-aux-Baronnie I taste a little more wine. It's perfectly acceptable, even though it's only 10:00 in the morning. I continue on my way. I'm slowing down; there's actually no wind now. If the wind was still blowing it would have been helping me along. Always something to whine about.

I turn off and stop, but this time for a glass of juice made from organic muscat grapes, maybe the most delicious drink I've ever tasted. Organic crops are now being cultivated even in the more conservative agricultural regions of France. They are probably under extreme pressure to do so, I can imagine.

Once more, I turn off the planned road because the traffic has become too heavy. I choose a good route, but it's somewhat difficult as the road climbs and climbs. If my breathing isn't enough of an indication, I just look around me. Nature is its own altimeter. First, the small plots of land with vegetables and flower beds start to disappear, then the vines and then the olive trees. In the end, it's only pine trees and scrubby evergreen oaks. The valley far below me looks like it could have been forgotten by the outside world, crouching behind Mont Ventoux. They probably speak their own language there and have never seen a blond cyclist before.

I buy a *pan bagnat* and a glass of rosé from a woman in a converted caravan parked next to a bend in a river. I remember that this egg and tuna sandwich was the only thing I ate during my first trip here by train. I continue on and I'm surrounded by lavender. There are lavender fields everywhere. All of the fields have just been harvested but still give off a faint whiff of old lady's wardrobe. The long, dense rows of small rounded plants in the fields make me think of lines of little waves in the sea. I can imagine how they would look if they were purple.

I decide to stay the night in Sault, which markets itself as the Capital of Lavender. Here, lavender is used for everything and is not only sold as bouquets and in fabric sachets, but is also used to flavour cakes and ice cream, and also honey made by bees who have collected the nectar from the lavender fields. By the way, eating lavender ice cream is rather like chewing on a bar of soap that has been kept in the freezer.

My hotel, Le Louvre, is nice and quite full, but it offers half board at an affordable price and bicycle storage is included. So I enjoy duck liver pâté, slow-cooked beef, a plate of cheese and some delicious wine from nearby Châteauneuf-du-Pape.

The next morning, while I'm waiting to check out, I browse through a book in the lobby by John Walsh and Hannah Reynolds, *France en Velo: The Ultimate Cycle Journey from Channel to Mediterranean – St. Malo to Nice.* The 20km (12 mile) stretch through the Gorge de la Nesque, they write, is the finest cycling road in the whole of France. Gorge de la Nesque, that's where I'm going next! Sometimes you get lucky.

"A very fine route," confirms the porter, "almost compulsory cycling."

And it is extremely nice. How the tiny river, more of a brook, has been able to cut such a deep ravine blows my mind. You have to really squint if you want to see the water all the way down the length of the gorge. But that doesn't make it any less beautiful. All the climbing I have done over the last two days is rewarded today with a long, not too steep downhill, the best kind.

It's not until I'm almost down that the vegetation starts changing again from the scrubby trees ideal for chamois and wild boar to hide in. Then the vines, vegetable gardens, beehives and flowers return, but above all, there are fruit trees. I'm greeted by a sign that reads "Welcome to The Cherry Valley." From the Capital of Lavender to The Cherry Valley, it sounds almost as beautiful as it is. Unfortunately, it's not cherry season now. The leaves wither in the heat like the ears of sad dogs.

Then I ride past vineyards that rarely get rave reviews, but that's okay. Here they produce the kind of wine we enjoy when buying it in boxes. Finally, I leave my rental bike, go to the pastry shop to buy a slice of cherry cake that I devour with a glass of rosé on the square in Bédoin. It goes well with that, too.

WINTER CYCLING I rent a room with a balcony in Sicily. Below me, there's a road and on the other side of the road, a narrow pebble beach and the Mediterranean. My room is on the top floor. On the floor below me, a woman lives with her family. Below her is her mother, who has rented me the room, and on the bottom floor there is a fish shop. Sometimes, in the morning when I make my coffee in the tiny kitchen and look out at the view, I see wet footprints coming out of the sea, continuing up the beach, crossing the road and the pavement and then going straight into the fish shop. The footprints are made by the owner of the shop who has been out snorkelling at dawn to catch squid with his harpoon. The owner told me that I don't have to drag my bike up the four flights of stairs, I can park it in the entrance of the building. I do so, but every time I have to remove the handlebars and turn them 90 degrees because the entrance is so narrow.

In the mornings I work and in the afternoon I cycle. Either a long ride along the coast or an unplanned adventure up Etna on more or less bike-friendly roads. It's January and the landscape is green and lush. Oranges and lemons hang on mature trees and lie in baskets along the roadside for shipping or selling on site.

Once, winter used to be high season for tourism here, as it was in Rome, Athens, Nice, Monaco and Capri. The summer was considered too hot, too dusty and too colourless. Then the obsession with bathing took hold, and that became the only reason to travel south and tourists stopped coming in the winter and began to come in the summer instead.

Above me, Taormina hangs on a cliff, a resort town that's been a tourist attraction since ancient times. In the winter it's quite empty, as is Giardino Naxos where I'm staying. The hotels are closed, as are most restaurants. Nevertheless, I can ride every day for a month. Sometimes it rains, but mostly not. I wear shorts every day and a thin windproof jacket. I ride to an outdoor café and then back again. Or to a vineyard. Or to an orange seller.

In the mornings, I sit on the balcony with a blanket around me, sip my coffee and watch the sun rise. In the evenings, I sit on the balcony with a blanket around me, sip a glass of wine and watch the lobster fisherman pass by with his bright light on the stern of his boat. One morning, I get a text from my eldest daughter asking if I saw Mount Etna erupt the night before? She read about it in the news. I did not. But when I sat there on the balcony, I noticed that Etna was glowing, and saw a stream of lava running down the side of the volcano. I get on the bike and ride uphill until I come to a fresh lava field. Black, sterile, unpleasant – it's smoking like someone has poured water over the coals in a sauna.

WOOL was the dominant material for both cycling jerseys and shorts for a long while. As with all materials, there was good and bad wool. Merino wool is one of the absolute best. Initially, merino wool came from southern Spain, possibly North Africa, and by the 18th century, it was forbidden to export merino sheep from the Iberian peninsula. Today, 80 percent of merino wool comes from Australia. When used in a base layer garment, merino wool is hard to beat, but when it comes to cycling clothes, it's only really bought by retro or environmentally conscious cyclists. Certainly, merino wool garments can be close fitting and elastic, but they don't really stay like that when exposed to moisture and weight. The combination of merino wool, rain, a few tools and a banana in your back pocket will soon result in your items dangling below the level of the saddle.

But merino wool still has one clear advantage in addition to its environmental superiority, which is that the material counteracts the smell of sweat. Remember that sweat itself doesn't smell. It's when bacteria on the skin break down the sweat that the odour

is released. Merino wool contains a substance, creatine, which instead breaks down these bacteria. It's a natural miracle fibre. That's why you can still wear your merino wool jersey after one or two, even three, sweaty rides while your synthetic jersey still smells even after you take it out of the washing machine. Therefore, for stylish café cycling, merino wool comes highly recommended. And no, it isn't itchy.

WORK There aren't a lot of jobs that involve cycling anymore. The knife-grinder of my childhood is no longer around. He parked his bike on the pavement and I'd bring down some knives to be sharpened. He had a grindstone that was attached to the bicycle frame between the saddle and the handlebars. He picked up his bike and hooked it in on a large support, a kind of cradle that left the rear wheel hanging in the air, and he began to pedal the bike. Instead of pushing the bike forward, the rear wheel now turned a leather strap on the frame which turned his grindstone.

In some countries, you can still find grinders and others who choose to use a bicycle to power a washing machine, a water pump, a goods elevator or a fruit juicer. The latter is not only found in poorer countries with relatively expensive electricity, but also in trendy gyms in the Western world.

Bicycle couriers who deliver both smaller packages and larger goods by bicycle are beginning to grow in number, though quite slowly. Every time I get a package delivered (having painstakingly made sure I've ordered the organic option) or the neighbour gets his eco-friendly box of fruit and vegetables, I'm surprised to see it arrive in a diesel vehicle. However, there's also a lot of new thinking about. Nowadays, I've seen coffins transported by bicycle, cycling nurses, cycling policemen and in the centre of London, an ambulance that seems to be a bicycle. Velocipede artists performing in circuses and cycling ice-cream and coffee sellers in parks are, of course, still around. In India, there are bicycle rickshaws carrying goods or passengers, and in Kenya, passengers can get a lift in padded cargo holders on bikes. And of course there are still cycling postmen.

Last but not least, the old, unrighteous profession in this two-wheeled industry: the bicycle thief. As the Irish writer Flann O'Brien said, "Why should anyone steal a wristwatch when he could steal a bicycle?"

X

THE X – full name the VeloX 3 – is the world's fastest bike. It is almost completely enclosed to form the most aerodynamic shape possible and the rider lies in an almost horizontal position. This two-wheeled bicycle has been clocked at a speed of 133.78kph (83mph).

XC, or cross country, is the name for cycling off road, straight through the terrain. The term is also used for running and skiing. XC is one of the disciplines under the umbrella of mountain biking and has been an Olympic sport since 1996.

XING is an abbreviation of "crossing", that is, when a cyclist moves through stationary traffic by continuously changing lanes.

Y

YPRES should really come under the letter "I", since the Flemish name of this city is Ieper. Still, few might have understood which city I was talking about. But now you know, I'm headed to Ypres.

Dries Verclyte, a cyclist working at the tourist office, points to the Textile Weavers' Hall – a huge, impressive baroque building – and he says:

"Newly built," after which he sweeps his arms, points to all the buildings around the big square and continues, "new, new, new."

Everything is new, built after the First World War. Germany paid for it. It was the Germans who had bombed Ypres into the ground. Literally. The Textile Weavers' Hall had been there since 1380, a visual reminder of how much you can earn making cloth, but also a memorial to a lost epoch. In 1383, Ypres was at war with Ghent, a war over the textile industry, one presumes, and never recovered.

"Everything was rebuilt after World War 1 just the way it was. Stone for stone. The Flemish are a tough and stubborn people – maybe that's why we like cycling."

We cycle out into the countryside. It doesn't take long. Ypres is a small town. It's quite easy riding along the small, winding roads. And winding they certainly are. Here, there weren't any land consolidation reforms to create order and ownership over the fields. The roads twist this way and that in pleasing curves, but sometimes at right angles. Taken at a fairly slow pace, this is a great road for cycling, but I can see that it's another matter if you are cycling in a race such as the Tour of Flanders. I understand that American cyclist George Hincapie described the race as follows: "It feels like a million bends, combined with 20 or 30 climbs and narrow roads, with no straight stretches longer than a few kilometres. All this makes it feel like a war on a bike. There is no race in North America comparable to this. The Tour of Flanders could just as well be a sport in its own right."

We cycle over grassy hills dotted with muscly beef cows, and beside fields of densely planted wheat and Brussels sprouts, which grow on remarkable plants. They look like little green palm trees with the tiny cabbage-like buds hanging on the trunks. It looks as if every little road we are cycling on is part of the Flemish cycle route network. Unlike most other cycling trails I've seen, the signs not only mark the routes, but each junction is marked with one or more numbers.

"We call them nodes," says Dries. "It was 1995, I think, that a retired mining engineer came up with this system. It was the same system they used underground to find their way around the mines."

Dries gets out his phone; of course, there's also an app for this (Google the words "*Fiets kompass*"; *fiets* means bicycle in Flemish).

"Have you seen this?" says Dries, showing me a map on his phone filled with loops and dots. "For example, if you do not want to cycle a whole route, you can remove a few nodes and the distance will be a bit shorter. Or, add some nodes to increase the length of your ride. If you create your own route by joining different nodes, then others can use it too. Do you see? Chocolate Tour. Café Tour. Beer Tour and Bird-watching Tour."

It's undeniably impressive. Not only that Europe's best cycle network exists and covers all of Flanders, but that it's constantly being updated and added to by cyclists.

"There are several thousand volunteers who keep it updated. Each person is assigned three streets in a town or three roads in the countryside. Then they report online if a sign is damaged or missing. Often the next day, it's fixed. The missing signs have often been swiped as souvenirs. If you name a route after Eddy Merckx, you can count on the signs being stolen."

Is there also a War Tour, I wonder? But I don't ask. In the same way that Vietnam wants to be regarded as a country and not a war, so it is with this part of Flanders. Dries has told me that

Ypres would prefer to be associated with future peace, but it's not easy to think of the future when passing field after field of graves with infinite lines of identical, anonymous white crosses. It's not easy when you read that there are still about half a million people missing. Some of these dead are found every time someone sinks a spade in the ground to build a new house. It's not easy when you have been reading books by Peter Englund, who describes one of these battles, no different than all the others, in this war of trenches. In a battle that lasted half a year, the British sacrificed hundreds of thousands of soldiers to advance their trench by just 8km (5 miles). And it was a piece of meaningless countryside which they abandoned a few months later.

"Have you noticed?" says Dries, changing the subject. "All the round ponds that the cows drink from. Those are granite pits that have been refilled. A bit bizarre."

We take a break at a café in a small town, and take our time studying an extensive beer menu before we choose.

"Here in Flanders, it's common for every café to have its own little bicycle club. At any rate, the café is the perfect place for a cycling club. Café and club, all in one."

"There's no problem with mixing cycling and alcohol?"

"Not at all."

Lucky for me, I think, and take another swig of a beer whose name I can't pronounce and will soon have forgotten. It's probably been made according to a mediaeval recipe in some dark, damp vault by a beer master who is a fourteenth generation descendant of a famous Trappist monk.

Back on our bikes, Dries tells me how the Flemish even like to watch cycling as a form of entertainment. It's a big thing. Basically, everyone cycles at weekends and commutes to work by bike. That's quite different from the Dutch who aren't so far away. It once again emphasizes that the way a population cycles is down to habit, a habit that can be changed if the will is there.

"We have tourists coming here to cycle. They come in four different varieties. Those who like to ride a bit while they are here. They hire a bike in town. Then there are those who bring their own bike, road bike or mountain bike, for some serious cycling. Next, there are those who have come on a cycling package holiday for a few days, a week maybe, and ride comfortably through the landscape while their luggage is being transported by car. And finally, those who pass through Flanders because they're cycling one of the longer cycle routes, like the EV4, the one that goes along the Atlantic coast."

"Down there," Dries says, "is a pub called In De Wulf. It's in an old converted farmhouse. It was selected as Europe's best restaurant recently. You can stay there, too. And over there, in that little village, a singer runs his own bike tour every spring. Belcantour is its name, of course."

Then we reach Kemmelberg and neither of us talks for a long time: it's cobblestones for 355m (388 yards) and a 13 percent average gradient, reaching as much as 23 percent. By the time we get to the top, I'm completely worn out. After that, it's an equally tough downhill run over even worse cobblestones. Down on the flat again, it feels like most of my body parts are out of place and need to be put back where they belong.

Finally, we cycle back to the new city of Ypres, which is a copy of the mediaeval city of Ypres. It's a little strange. As if nothing had happened. But what do I know about war and how best to go on after homes and towns have been ruined? I who grew up in a country that holds the world record for peace.

Z

THE ZEDLER INSTITUT for bicycle technology and safety is a fairly unusual independent test centre for bicycles. The test results are often published in the German journals *Tour*, for road bikes, and *Bike*, for mountain bikes.

ZIPP manufactures bicycle parts. The company is primarily known for its wheels, especially its disc wheels.